DATE DUE

NO 30 '92			
JA 8 '93			
RENEW			
JE 18 '93			
FE 10 '94			
AP 22 '94			
JE 30 '94			
NO 18 '94			
DE 9 '94			
RENEW			
AP 21 '95			
DE 8 '95			
OC 19 '99			
MY 3 '00			
AP 7 '03			

DEMCO 38-296

Marketing Without Mystery

A Practical Guide to Writing a Marketing Plan

Laura M. Dirks
Sally H. Daniel

amacom
American Management Association

This book is available at a special discount when ordered in bulk quantities. For information, contact Special Sales Department, AMACOM, a division of American Management Association, 135 West 50th Street, New York, NY 10020.

Library of Congress Cataloging-in-Publication Data

Dirks, Laura M.
Marketing without mystery : a practical guide to writing a marketing plan / Laura M. Dirks, Sally H. Daniel.
p. cm.
Includes bibliographical references and index.
ISBN 0-8144-7764-X (paperback)
1. Marketing—Management. 2. Marketing—Planning. I. Daniel, Sally H. II. Title.
HF5415.13.D49 1991
658.8'02—dc20 *91-19870*
CIP

Printing number

10 9 8 7 6 5 4 3 2 1

To the men in our lives
who taught us to follow our hearts
to uncover the mysteries of the business world—
our fathers, **Mac** and **Red,**
and our husbands, **Dave** and **Bill**

Contents

List of Planning Exercises

Preface

We all want good information, fast and in usable form. In our personal searches for the answers to our own marketing questions, we have found that a lot of technical information about marketing is hidden in texts. There is much good information, but a lot of it is hard to locate or buried in line after line of explanation.

We know that people have different learning styles and that the majority of us learn through a combination of styles. In *Marketing Without Mystery*™, we present technical material in a format that is both easily accessible and readily understood and that takes into account each of the basic learning modes.

Included are:

- Clear, concise explanations of how to put your plan on paper for presentation
- Detailed but simple explanations of how to complete a marketing budget
- Format indentations that allow listing of important facts
- Visual charts, graphs, and drawings that show the relationship among theories
- A text written in easily understood language
- Ample white space for your notes
- A detailed table of contents
- Planning exercises for interactive responses and analyses
- Strategic playsheets for examining marketing options
- An appendix of frequently needed research sources with addresses and telephone numbers
- A workbook format that allows you to interact with, discuss, and repeat material on different aspects of the marketing process as many times as needed

Marketing Without Mystery™ was originally developed as a series of worksheets based on traditional marketing concepts. The intent was to provide a structured, yet simple, method for teaching the entire marketing process. As we presented these worksheets in seminars for entrepreneurs and marketing professionals, we realized that a visual presentation was most effective as a teaching device. As a result of both our own experience and the many requests we have received from seminar participants, we decided to reformat these seminar materials into easy-to-use interactive strategic playsheets that provide guidance in developing information about your company, about target markets, and about the products and services you plan to offer to the target markets. As you add more target markets and develop more strategies for serving them, you build on your initial marketing plan; the completed strategic playsheets can then become the basis for an organized marketing plan.

The interactive format of the playsheets invites you to play with different marketing ideas for your business in a creatively organized manner. We have chosen the term *playsheet* because we want you to experiment with selecting, analyzing, and evaluating your marketing options. According to Webster's dictionary, one definition of *play* is "to direct the course of." To *play the game* is defined as "to act according to a code or set of standards." We encourage you to utilize this book both to play with marketing options and to play the game of marketing planning skillfully in order to manage your opportunities and increase your profits.

You will discover that marketing planning is a very powerful business tool. Although some consider it an optional tool, marketing influences and changes people's perceptions about your business, products, services, or ideas. Therefore, you must use it with integrity. You will also discover that there really is no mystery to the marketing process.

Who Should Read This Book

Marketing Without Mystery™ is an action-oriented reference for the entrepreneur, product manager, or other marketing professional who wants to reduce the risks of offering products and services to customers. For those who do not have an extensive marketing background, it is also a practical, inexpensive way to learn about marketing planning while advancing your knowledge about your own business or project.

The information in this book has helped hundreds of entrepreneurs, marketing planners, and students learn the marketing process and apply that process to developing marketing plans for products and services in today's competitive environment. Sound marketing theory is united with practical, process-oriented checklists, outlines, figures, and strategic playsheets to focus on the end product—marketing strategies to help move your business forward.

Marketing is a dynamic subject. However, the planning process remains static. This book is a basic primer for developing simple marketing plans. It is neither a detailed reference nor a text but a working book to enable you to begin your planning processes.

How to Use This Book

If you are a novice to the concepts of marketing, we recommend that you walk through each chapter of the book. You may want to pick one of your products or services and use the **planning exercises** in the order presented, then repeat the exercises for your other products or services.

If you're already somewhat familiar with the overall marketing process but want information about a specific part, turn to the relevant section and work through the chapter until you have your answers or at least know which questions to research.

Many entrepreneurs, product managers, and marketing professionals have requested outlines and forms for writing a simple marketing plan. If this is your need, turn to Chapter 11, which discusses different approaches to writing a marketing plan.

The External and Internal Situation

1

Marketing: Ready or Not?

Marketing represents the creative part of your business. It is a process for managing your company's assets in order to identify markets and meet customer needs at a profit. Through this process, you learn how to review your options creatively and select those that best fit your company's overall goals.

To begin the marketing process, you should review the background and competitive environment of your company as well as any factors that may limit your organization's options. You should then select and analyze target markets and match the following 4 Ps to each market's needs:

1. Product-Service Mix
2. Price Mix
3. Place-Distribution Mix
4. Promotion Mix

For each target market, a marketing strategy mix that meets your company's objectives must be developed. Your marketing plan comprises all these strategies.

Technically, then, marketing is a process for analyzing, planning, and managing your organization's resources while identifying and serving current and potential client groups and their needs profitably.

Reasons for Introducing the Marketing Process

Company managers choose to introduce and/or reemphasize marketing planning for a number of reasons, which may range from personal interest to corporate policy. However, the reason usually centers around an opportunity or an identified problem that the company management needs to explore. Examples include:

- Introducing new products or services
- Expanding into new markets
- Differentiating products or services
- Revitalizing products, services, or markets
- Deleting or "demarketing" products, services, or markets
- Responding to a drop in sales or profits
- Responding to aggressive competition
- Evaluating financial or legal risks of opportunities

- Motivating employees
- Enhancing company image or reputation

Planning Exercise 1-1.
Why Marketing Planning? Why Now?

Why is marketing planning necessary for your company at this time? State your company's most important reasons for preparing a marketing plan as you see them.

1. ______________________________
2. ______________________________
3. ______________________________

Guidelines for Marketing Planning

As a practical matter, you want to introduce the marketing process in a manner that helps you reduce your planning risks and increase your chance of success. Although there are no hard and fast rules, the following general guidelines are worth considering:

1. Have a stated, clear vision of what you ultimately hope to achieve over the long term. This vision, often called a mission statement, reflects your company's philosophy or purpose.

2. Establish goals and objectives for your company as a whole. Goals are broad statements about management's intentions, areas of emphasis, or key issues facing the company. Marketing objectives are specific, measurable statements of what will be accomplished, by when, and how the success of the marketing plan will be measured.

3. Make sure the objectives for your plan are measurable and easy to communicate. The simpler they are, the better, because more people will be able to understand and (you hope) support them. Even if the vision and goals for the company are fuzzy, each marketing plan should have specific objectives. We discuss developing marketing objectives in Chapter 4.

4. The actual development of each plan should be the responsibility of the individual or group that will direct its implementation and that will be judged by the plan's results. There's nothing like a vested interest to help ensure success.

5. The plan should be in writing and should be approved by the division head, CEO, or board of directors, whichever is ultimately responsible for the success of the company.

6. Each plan should have a built-in review date at which preliminary measurements are taken and any necessary adjustments to the plan are made. Be willing to re-evaluate your market, and be flexible as additional research and information become available.

Marketing: Ready or Not?

If you've read this far, you already have some key information about your company and about your possibilities for using marketing planning. Congratulations! Welcome to the *Marketing Without Mystery*™ process.

Planning Exercise 1-2.
Vision

State your company's vision for the future. In what areas do you want to make a difference? (This statement will be refined in Chapter 2.)

VISION STATEMENT for (company name) ________________________________

____

____

____

Planning Exercise 1-3.
Goals

State the goals from your company's business plan. Goals are generally set forth broadly and involve action. Your company's marketing goals may be to profitably introduce, serve, expand, or develop a particular product or service for one or more markets. These goals will be used in Chapter 4 to establish specific objectives for your marketing plan.
List all of the goals for your company here and check only those that relate to marketing issues.

GOALS
Broad statements of intent:

If these goals concern marketing, check here:

1. ____

____

2. ____

____

3. ____

____

4. ____

____

5. ____

____

You will be developing separate marketing plans for achieving each marketing goal. Circle one or two goals that will be the focus of this marketing plan. Additional goals can be identified and marketing plans developed to achieve them at a later date.

Planning Exercise 1-4.
Responsibility

Write the name and title of the person responsible for writing and carrying out this marketing plan.

Name: ______________________ Title: ______________________

Who needs to approve this plan?

Name: ______________________ Title: ______________________

What is your time frame for implementing this plan? Most marketing plans are for short-run projects or programs, e.g., those that run from three to twelve months.

Start date: ______________________ Completion date: ______________________

When is a logical time to review your progress—after one or six months, or after a particular phase of your project is completed?

Review dates: ____

Complete Playsheet 1, the Cover Page, for your marketing plan.

STRATEGIC PLAYSHEET 1.

Example Cover Page

MARKETING PLAN
for

Company name: *XYZ Corporation*

prepared by

Name, title: *Sam Smith, Product Manager*

Date: *January 1993*

approved by

Name, title: *Dave Jones, Marketing VP*

Date: *February 1993*

Review date: *June 1993*

STRATEGIC PLAYSHEET 1.

Cover Page

MARKETING PLAN
for

Company name: ______________________________

prepared by

Name, title: ______________________________

Date: ______________________________

approved by

Name, title: ______________________________

Date: ______________________________

Review date: ______________________________

2

Marketing: A Focus for the Future

The key thing to remember when you develop a marketing plan is that each combination of company, product, service, and market mix—and, therefore, each plan—is unique. What worked for another company may or may not work for yours.

Your company should have a stated, clear vision of what you hope to achieve in the long term. It is important to keep your company's vision in mind as you go through the planning process; it will guide you as you research and evaluate your many possibilities for serving your customers—at a profit.

What Your Business Really Is

What is your *real* business? Think in broad terms. Your real business is a combination of:

- The products and services your company offers
- Your broadened vision or scope of that offer
- The benefits that you provide to your customers or target markets

Your real business is often more dynamic and interesting than the business you think you have. The more you focus on what you do for your clients and customers, the greater your possibilities for further business become. For example, consider the questions these businesses asked themselves:

- *CPAs.* Do we provide financial statements and tax returns? Or do we really provide the security and peace of mind that comes from our clients' knowing their financial affairs are in order?
- *Cosmetic Companies.* Do we sell lipstick? Or do we offer hope of greater style or sex appeal?
- *Photographers.* Do we provide only photos? Or do we preserve memories and enhance reality?

Examine the examples of products shown in Figure 2-1, their broadened vision, and the benefits they offer their customers. See how their real business is broadened by the company vision.

Figure 2-1. Broadened Vision—Business Examples.

Product-Service	*Broadened Vision*	*Benefits*
Passenger airline	provides not just transportation	but convenient, fast travel that's adventurous and fun.
Pudding	offers not just a snack or dessert	but a treat that's good for you and fun to eat.
Shampoo	embodies not just head care	but a glamorous life-style.
Paper plates	are not just disposable products	but color-coordinated, and now biodegradable, conveniences.
Orange juice	is not just natural food	but a drink loaded with vitamins, minerals, and now even calcium.

Defining Your Company's Vision

All companies have a purpose in addition to making a profit, but often that purpose is not clearly thought out or stated. Defining your own vision is important because it tells people who you are and what you do. You should measure your many marketing options against this vision statement; it provides the focus for your planning process. Later, you may want to tie your promotion to your vision through a slogan that reflects your purpose. The following examples of vision statements for several companies provide a future-focused guide for today's actions. They are based on the company's product-service mix plus its broadened vision, which together provide a desired future result.

Vision Statement Examples

A *COMMUNITY SCHOOL* empowers all children and adults to improve their lives through quality education.

A *CONSULTING COMPANY* assists women-influenced businesses through business education seminars.

A *PUBLISHING COMPANY* expands life through books.

A *TOY SHOP* educates children and parents through play.

An *AUTOMOBILE SERVICE STATION* protects lives by ensuring the mechanical safety of automobiles.

In all companies, the corporate vision is defined by the management group. Find out what its vision is, and use it to align your marketing plan. If the vision is not stated and it is your responsibility to help define it, Planning Exercises 2-1 and 2-2 may be helpful as you articulate your company's view of its purpose.

Planning Exercise 2-1.
Your Company's Vision

1. Take a few minutes to think about your company's vision and its real purpose, which you noted in Chapter 1.
2. Repeat the process for your company's vision for the future. In what areas do you want to make a difference?

   Vision Statement for (company name) ______________________________

   ____

   ____

3. The vision statement needs to be broad enough to cover all of your company's goals and objectives for its future direction. Don't limit your dreams. Think of the vision as an umbrella under which your various marketing plans will operate.

   What do you see for your company in five years? ____________________

   ____

   ____

Planning Exercise 2-2.
Refining Your Company Vision

1. Describe your company in two or three words. If there are several people working with you to develop your vision, have each person select two or three descriptive words.

An accounting firm listed:	Write your words here:
conscientious	____________________
professional	____________________
efficient	____________________
personal	____________________
responsive	____________________
service-oriented	____________________
personal	____________________

2. Combine those words or essences to form a definition of your company. It may be rough at this point; you can fine-tune it before you write your plan. The accounting firm used the words listed in item 1 to come up with this sentence:

> A conscientious, professional, and service-oriented CPA firm that provides personal and efficient service in the areas of tax preparation, financial services management, financial statement preparation and review.

Write your combined descriptive words here: ______________________________

____

____

3. Your customers categorize your operations based on their reactions to what services you do and do not provide and how information is communicated to them. Take this opportunity to conduct some basic research by asking your customers and employees to list a few words that come to mind when they think of your company.

Option 1

Provide a 3- by 5-inch card on which the customer or employee may write the descriptive words and ask the respondents to put the cards in a designated box so that the comments are anonymous. Do not be judgmental when evaluating the responses.

> ***Customer's Vision of Your Business***
>
> Please help us with some market research for our company. On this card, list three words that describe our company.
>
> 1.______________________________
>
> 2.______________________________
>
> 3.______________________________
>
> You do not need to put your name on this card. Just drop it in the box at the door. Thank you for your help.

Option 2

You can use a guestbook to solicit comments and obtain continuous feedback from your customers. The guestbook can also serve other research functions; for example, it can help you build a mailing list. Because guestbooks do not provide anonymity, customers' responses may not be entirely candid.

4. Compare the client responses to your other responses. What did you learn? Is their view the same as yours? Either a yes or a no answer gives you a great deal of information.

Marketing: A Focus for the Future

On the next pages, you will refine your own vision as you complete Strategic Playsheet 2. Having conducted some research and broadened your vision for your company, you already have a new way of looking at your company, organization, project, product, or service.

STRATEGIC PLAYSHEET 2.

Example Vision Statement

Now, rewrite your vision in one or two sentences in the space below. Remember that you want to provide a future-focused guide for today's actions. [*Remember that the descriptive sentence for the accounting firm was "A conscientious, professional, and service-oriented CPA firm that provides personal and efficient service in the areas of tax preparation, financial services management, and financial statement preparation and review."*]

Vision Statement *A C.P.A. firm provides not just tax returns but also conscientious, professional, personal financial preparation and management services for companies and individuals.*

Refined Vision Statement for ____________ Company ____________

[*Your vision statement provides a future-focused guide for today's actions. Base your refined vision on your product-service mix plus your broadened vision of the company's purpose.*]

We are a CPA firm that protects companies and individuals through conscientious, professional, personal financial preparation and management services.

STRATEGIC PLAYSHEET 2.

Vision Statement

Now, rewrite your vision in one or two sentences in the space below. Remember that you want to provide a future-focused guide for today's actions.

Vision Statement ____

____

____

____

Refined Vision Statement for ____________________ Company ____________________

____

____

____

3

Background: Your Business and Its Environment

Like people, businesses should not operate in a vacuum. They must interact with the world around them in order to grow.

We each know that there are things we can and cannot do. Similarly, corporations can adjust their strategies to become more profitable. An organization and the individuals in it have a responsibility to use their opportunities for profit in a responsible and ethical way.

Ethics is not the only limitation that a company encounters as it plans for profitability. There are many others, both external and internal, that impose boundaries on your company's operations.

This chapter shows you how to set parameters to help determine your marketing plan. Among these parameters are a number of factors external to your company, such as the business environment in which it operates, and various internal factors that influence your marketing decisions and the strategies you adopt to meet your objectives.

External Boundaries

Encircling our companies externally are situations we cannot change easily. These include the environments that our companies exist in, including:

- Political and legal environment
- Cultural and social environment
- Economic environment
- Technological environment
- Competitive environment
- Industrial environment

These limiting factors set the parameters within which our companies must function; they set the stage for our existence. In order to operate optimally, we must be aware of these boundaries and monitor them so that we remain within the circle they form. At the same time, we can push to expand these boundaries in order to increase our opportunities.

In the real business world, you must weigh the effects of externally dictated factors on your company. Barring catastrophic events, these environments are slow to change, and it is difficult to alter them within a short period of time. One obvious exception is the technological environment.

You should review each environment briefly and assess its potential impact on your marketing decisions.

- *Political and Legal Environment.* Over the years, laws have been enacted to encourage competition and to protect small businesses and consumers from potentially unethical practices. In addition, states and cities impose licensing fees and sales tax requirements for many types of businesses and products or services. Many industries with special interests and/or their trade associations hire lobbyists or governmental representatives to monitor and influence these environments.
- *Cultural and Social Environment.* This factor sets the parameters for what is culturally and socially expected and acceptable in your area. These factors are usually based on tradition and may stem from such influences as religion, ethnicity, life-style, and geographic location. Because societal values are slow to change, companies must recognize and work within the standards set by the community.
- *Economic Environment.* Economic considerations are grouped into three basic areas: country, region, and city. Each influences your market's ability to purchase and, therefore, your profitability. In recent years, the economic environment has changed more frequently than formerly. Because economic change has increased, monitoring this environment is imperative for most companies.
- *Technological Environment.* As the rate at which new technology is developed increases, your options multiply. Because the increase is so rapid, it mandates changes in the way you plan and conduct your business. This environment can dramatically impact your markets as well as your business.
- *Competitive Environment.* As you analyze your competition, you will identify windows of opportunity for your business. Be assured that you are not the only company monitoring its competition. As obvious business opportunities become increasingly few as a result of increases in both the number and the kinds of companies competing for business, it will become necessary to search harder for hidden potential.
- *Industrial Environment.* This environment has developed two conflicting trends in recent years: (1) a trend toward increasing cooperation within industries through trade associations and other coalitions and (2) a trend toward consolidation, takeovers, and fierce competition within industries. It is most important that you identify which trend your industry tends to follow, because this environment sets the stage for most of your marketing planning decisions. Much of your market's perceptions and expectations about conducting business with your company are based on the image and reputation of your industry—its policies and general ethics.

Internal Boundaries

Companies guide and focus marketing planning decisions by limiting directions and setting internal boundaries, such as:

- Internal resources
- Goals and objectives
- Ethics, both personal and corporate

Internally directed factors are those your company management sets and that form the company environment. This category covers all your marketing planning activities, including budgeting and implementation. The decisions that the management of your corporation makes enable you to tell both your employees and your entire network who you are and where you want to go with your business.

- *Internal Resources.* This factor comprises capacity, equipment, inventory, manpower, money, and goodwill. How your company chooses to use these resources reveals its priorities. You are expected to develop and implement strategies that make the best use of the company's resources and provide profits for continued development. Your product's marketing plans may directly compete with your company's other products for resources and budget allotments.
- *Company Goals and Objectives.* Goals set the direction for both long- and short-term gains and therefore determine the focus and strategies of your marketing plan. It is within the specific environment of your company that your marketing plans must be developed and implemented.
- *Corporate Ethics.* Codes of conduct for dealing with others determine corporate reference groups and networks, including customers, suppliers, and employees. The ethical environment may enhance what you are able to do with your marketing plans; when the corporate standards for ethics and your personal standard of ethics are in alignment with the ethical expectations of your markets and those of your industry, you are more likely to develop successful strategies to serve your markets and profit your company and yourself.

The Business Environment and Your Marketing Plan

Knowledge of your company's external and internal limitations may lead you to better strategic decisions. It may even be that a change within your company or within the business environment has led you to think more seriously about your marketing plan.

All marketing plans should include an introductory section that provides summaries of both external and internal environments. This "situation analysis" is useful for benchmark studies and may include such things as:

- A brief history of your company or your division and its current status, done through an analysis of external limitations and internal resources
- The rationale that brought you to develop this plan (perhaps dictated by your management)
- An analysis of your major competitors in the market(s) under consideration

Company History and Goals

This section of the marketing plan usually includes a short paragraph about the history of your company.

> Our company is an old, established, family-owned business founded in 1909 by a father and son. . . .
>
> Our company [division] is one of many smaller businesses owned by a holding corporation. . . .
>
> We are a new company started in 1990 by two sisters in their basements. . . .

You should state your company's goals broadly and in action terms: "in order to profitably serve the dry goods needs of the pioneers," "to profitably expand the corporation's line of products," "to profitably make stained glass windows for owners of condominiums."

External Limitations

This section should detail any external factors that may have an impact on the marketing plan. We suggest that you review the following areas as you prepare to develop your plan:

Political and legal notes	Technological advances
Cultural and social expectations	Competitive situation
Economic factors	Personal, corporate, and industry ethics

The external factors often can provide some of the most productive opportunities. Be careful not to miss these opportunities. They may be important as you make your marketing decisions. In each of the following external areas, notice those that have changed or are likely to change soon and consider these questions:

- Will these changes provide opportunities or limitations for your products and services and for your markets?
- Which of these areas is most important to your company?
- Are any of these factors the main reason for this marketing plan? If so, note that changes in these areas are very costly and take a long time to make.

Political and Legal Notes

- Are there any specific changes in the law that affect your company?
- Are there legal or political areas that affect your clients and their relationship with your company?
- Can you help your markets become aware of recent political trends and legal changes and use them to their advantage? This kind of educational aid can provide strategies for marketing your products and services and can build strong ties with your markets.

Cultural and Social Expectations

- Describe the culture within which your business operates.
- Do your products or services and their markets dictate strict, formal negotiations?

- Do they lend themselves to more casual contacts and contracts? Are there any specific taboos?
- What is expected of businesses within your geographic area and your industry?

Economic Factors

- What are the general economic trends for the areas in which you offer your products and services?
- Do these trends affect your clients and potential clients? How?

Technological Factors

- What role does technology play in your business?
- Is the technology changing quickly, or is it static?
- Do you anticipate that technological advances will make your products and services more or less desirable to your markets in the future? Why?
- Do you anticipate technical changes that may help either you or your competition?
- If so, do you need to update your equipment? At what cost?

Competitive Situation

- Who are your closest competitors?
- Who serves the same markets as yours?
- Who offers similar products or services?
- Who is using the same suppliers?
- How much do you know about their businesses?
- How can you use this information to identify windows for your company?

Personal, Corporate, and Industry Ethics

- Does your company or industry have a stated code of ethics?
- What standards of personal and corporate behavior are expected?
- Are your personal values in alignment with those of the company?
- Is the company accountable to its customers for its products and services? Those involved in the marketing process are often seen as keepers of business ethics. Businesses can use the marketing process as a very powerful tool for persuading current and potential customers to accept their point of view; marketing managers should acknowledge this responsibility.

For more information on specific resources, see the Sources of Information section and the discussion in Chapter 12 of research and information gathering. Local and state chambers of commerce have economic data available for businesses to use in planning, and universities and colleges publish newsletters and articles on leading economic trends and their likely impact. You should either get on their mailing lists or use their libraries.

Planning Exercise 3-1.
External Limitations

Are there any external factors that may limit your company's ability to offer your products and services? If so, is there a way to turn that limitation into a competitive plus for your company or for its target markets? Write your notes here.

Political and Legal Notes ______________________________

____

____

Cultural and Social Expectations ______________________________

____

____

Economic Factors ______________________________

____

____

Technological Advances ______________________________

____

____

Industrial Climate ______________________________

____

____

Personal and Corporate Ethics ______________________________

____

____

STRATEGIC PLAYSHEET 3.

Example History and Goals for *Play Thinks* **Company**

Fill in a summary of your company's history here.

Our company has been in business since 1982. We are a family-owned business that manufactures educational toys and games. The goal of this plan is to increase our market share in the toy industry by introducing a computerized globe and corresponding atlas.

Fill in your goals and objectives here. Use only the major marketing goals that were checked in Chapter 1.

1. *to increase market share*
2. *to profitably introduce leading-edge educational toys*
3.
4.

STRATEGIC PLAYSHEET 3.

History and Goals for ________________ Company

Fill in a summary of your company's history here. ______________________________

Fill in your goals and objectives here. Use only the major marketing goals that were checked in Chapter 1.

1. ______________________________
2. ______________________________
3. ______________________________
4. ______________________________

Internal Resources

It is important to assess whether your company has the resources necessary to do the proposed projects. Consider the following questions about your internal resources. For each question, consider best- and worst-case scenarios.

Planning Exercise 3-2.

Internal Resource Analysis for ______________________ Company

Manpower

How many people are employed by your company? ______________

Are additional trained people available? ______________

If yes, how many are available for short-term projects? ______________

For long-term projects? ______________

How many people do you need to carry out your plan?

Maximum # ______________ Minimum # ______________

Do they have the skills to carry out the marketing plans?

Yes ______________ Maybe ______________ No ______________

If not, can they be trained in the necessary areas?

Yes ______________ Maybe ______________ No ______________

What special expertise does your company offer? ______________

____

What special expertise will you need to obtain? ______________

____

Is it readily available? ______________

At what cost? ______________

Money

What is the budgeting process for marketing activities? ______________

____

What are your financial resources for this project?

Best case ______________ Worst case ______________

What are your company's profit goals? ______________________

How much do you need to net for this project to be considered a success? __________

____

Time

What is your time frame for this project?

Best case ______________ Worst case ______________

Does your company plan well in advance or work on time crunches? __________

____

Are you dependent on other suppliers that may have time constraints of their own?

____

What kind of back-up arrangements can be made if your time lines are not met?

____

Materials

What are your resources? ______________________

Are supplies readily available, or are they scarce? ______________________

What quality and quantity are used? ______________________

Do you have alternate suppliers available? ______________________

What is your working arrangement with them? ______________________

After reviewing the above factors, circle the areas in which you believe your company is truly excellent. Which of these resources are not available from other companies? An element of excellence or a feature that is shared with no other company is called a distinctive advantage. It is this distinctive advantage that will provide windows of opportunity for your company.

STRATEGIC PLAYSHEET 4.

Example Distinctive Advantage for *Infocus Management Consulting* **Company**

A distinctive advantage is a unique area of excellence that your company has and that it may use to its advantage.

On the basis of the analysis of your internal resources, list the distinctive advantages of your company.

Manpower *eight consultants, twenty-five staff experienced in executive image development, public relations, speech development/public speaking*

Money *steady cash flow; owner-occupied building; no mortgage; large line of credit available from bank*

Time *large staff ensures immediate response to clients*

Materials *resources include expertise; track record with attendant data for previous fifteen years; video and training facilities*

STRATEGIC PLAYSHEET 4.

Distinctive Advantage for ____________________ Company

A distinctive advantage is a unique area of excellence that your company has and that it may use to its advantage.

On the basis of the analysis of your internal resources, list the distinctive advantages of your company.

Manpower ____

____

____

____

Money ____

____

____

Time ____

____

____

Materials ____

____

____

____

Rationale

Briefly state why you are doing this marketing plan, why it is important to your company, and why senior management should support it.

Your explanation of the rationale for your plan may refer to your company's history, a competitive strategy, requests from customers, or a wish to reaffirm goals. Your specific marketing plan objectives and a summary of your strategies should also be included here. (These concepts will be developed in Chapters 4 and 5.) Sample rationale statements used for marketing plans include:

> We are developing a marketing plan to unite our marketing efforts in the face of competition from discount department stores moving into our region.
>
> This marketing plan is required for the preparation of the company's annual budget.
>
> We are writing our marketing plan because we have few resources, we need to be efficient, and we are excited but scared about starting a new business.

STRATEGIC PLAYSHEET 5.

Example Rationale for Marketing Plan for *Adventure Computers* **Company**

Write a sentence or two that explains what brought you to develop this plan:

We are preparing to introduce a new product that will cost the company approximately $150,000. We want to minimize our risks and maximize our possibilities for success.

STRATEGIC PLAYSHEET 5.

Rationale for Marketing Plan for ____________________ Company

Write a sentence or two that explains what brought you to develop this plan: ____________

Competition

Most of us are used to competition in the world of sports, where contests are open and direct. In business, competition can be different. There aren't as many stories of David defeating Goliath in a head-to-head battle. Of course, David had to find Goliath's weakness to defeat him.

Although you may not always think so, competition is often more helpful than harmful to your business. Competitors help your business by:

- Increasing knowledge about your industry's products and services
- Expanding the uses for your products and services within the marketplace
- Defining your windows of opportunity—markets that are not being served by your competition

An analysis of your competition can identify some of your greatest opportunities. When you have studied your competition, you can go into a market with some knowledge. Competitors may have defined their markets, and, in doing so, left open windows of opportunity for your company to occupy and serve.

Try to pick up on any trends in your industry. A trend is a pattern of behavior that gathers momentum and develops consistency as time passes; a fad interests many people for a short while, loses momentum, and dies quickly. Because it takes a certain amount of time to develop and implement a marketing plan, your company should try to latch onto trends and avoid fads. Look at your competition to see how it is addressing the trends you have identified. As you match the trends to the competitive analysis, take note of any windows of opportunity that might be profitable for your company.

As you study your competitors, think about the following questions. They will help you identify one or more windows of opportunity your company might try to develop, if it believes the venture will be profitable.

- Are there markets that are not being served?
- Are there products that are underdeveloped?
- Are needed products nonexistent?
- Is a price range missing?
- What better ways do you have to place or distribute your products and services?
- How can your promotion tell your target markets about your distinctive advantage?

If competitive information is not readily available, study your industry's data, which are available through trade journals, trade associations, federal and state government reports, and special editions of some magazines. Chapter 12, on research and information gathering, lists specific references and how to contact them. Start and keep updated files on each competitor.

Planning Exercise 3-3.
Competitive Analysis

In the following table, compare each competitor, including your company, by stating and rating its marketing performance in each of the 4 Ps of its marketing mix. List each competitor's major markets, products and services, price ranges, placement and distribution of products, promotion methods, and gross sales. If a company offers multiple products that compete with each other, include each of them in the competitive analysis.

Identifying Windows of Opportunity

Major Competitor	*Market Served*	*Main Product or Service*	*Price Range*	*Placement and Distribution*	*Promotion Methods & Results*	*Gross Sales*
Name Address Industry Code* Strengths Weaknesses						
Name Address Industry Code* Strengths Weaknesses						
Name Address Industry Code* Strengths Weaknesses						
Name Address Industry Code* Strengths Weaknesses						

*Industry Code refers to SIC code, defined in Sources of Information

Have you uncovered any trends? List them. ______________________________

____

Are there any "holes" in the above competitive analysis that show areas that are not being served? ______________________________

____

These questions will identify one or more windows of opportunity for your company to consider developing. Circle them, and analyze which, if any, are worth the time and effort to pursue.

Figure 3-1. Strategy development options based on competitive analysis.

Size of Your Company	*Possible Strategy Options*	*Probable Competitive Reactions*
Small Company ▪ 1–2 products ▪ employees <20* ▪ minimum overhead ▪ owner-managed	Identify windows of opportunity. Go after small market segments not being served.	If the market is small, larger companies may find it too costly to serve and will leave you alone. If the market is large or very profitable, you will generate competition. Your edge may be your ability to move quickly and keep overhead low.
Medium Company ▪ 5–10 products ▪ employees <500* ▪ established identity ▪ more overhead ▪ may be owner-managed or directed	Still work with the profitable windows of opportunity. Service markets only partially served by competition. Look to exploit your distinctive advantage. Possibly start small, direct competitive drive, but be prepared for a strong competitive move. Watch overhead and other resources.	If the market is large and profitable, competition may develop new product or service for this market. If competition cannot develop new products before you are well-established, or if the market is only marginally profitable, it may leave you alone. If you start head-to-head competition, other companies will react.
Large Company ▪ multi-divisional ▪ employees >500* ▪ well-established identity ▪ considers other large companies major competition	Position your own products to compete with each other. If competition is about even with you, you may use the element of surprise to go after its markets.	Competition of similar size may surprise you with direct head-to-head drive for your markets. Direct competition costly. Large companies will weigh benefits against costs. Unless this market is very important to maintain other markets, it may leave you alone. However, be watchful.

*U.S. Small Business Administration designations.

Strategy Development

Study your analysis of the major competitors, and evaluate their strengths and weaknesses. Compare those strengths and weaknesses to your own company's list. In which areas are you stronger or filling a niche within your markets' needs? This is your window of opportunity for strategy development. Consider ways in which the competition serves or does not serve this market and how it may react as you select strategies to use your windows of opportunity (see Figure 3-1).

Identify yourself on this chart. Then identify your options and their anticipated results.

STRATEGIC PLAYSHEET 6.

Example Strategic Options for The Board Room Company
Analysis of Competition

The product under consideration for this plan is a skateboard. In this product area, we are a small-sized company. Listed below are our strategic options, our major competitors, and their anticipated reaction to each of our strategic options.

SPECIFIC STRATEGIC OPTIONS	COMPETITORS	ANTICIPATED REACTIONS
1. *custom design skateboards*	*none locally except do-it-yourselfers*	*none initially*
2. *sell accessories*	*sporting goods stores*	*not much unless we advertise this service heavily*
3.		
4.		
5.		

From a competitive standpoint, which option appears to be most in your company's favor? Circle it.

STRATEGIC PLAYSHEET 6.

Example Strategic Options for ______________ Company
Analysis of Competition

The product under consideration for this plan is ____________. In this product area, we are a ________-sized company. Listed below are our strategic options, our major competitors, and their anticipated reaction to each of our strategic options.

SPECIFIC STRATEGIC OPTIONS	COMPETITORS	ANTICIPATED REACTIONS
1.		
2.		
3.		
4.		
5.		

From a competitive standpoint, which option appears to be most in your company's favor? Circle it.

STRATEGIC PLAYSHEET 7.

Example Environmental Situation Summary for *Custom Western* **Company**

Briefly summarize your areas of distinctive advantage. State what you have learned about your competition that will influence this plan. Specifically, which windows of opportunity will you seek to fill with this plan? What external factors affect this plan? What internal factors affect this plan?

Most cowboy boots are now manufactured by mass production. Custom-designed ones are not available locally but are becoming increasingly popular. Therefore, our opportunity is to design and sell a custom boot in our area. All materials are readily available, and the trend toward Western attire has triggered special orders from our customers.

NOTE: You will develop specific objectives and strategies for this plan in Chapters 4 and 5.

STRATEGIC PLAYSHEET 7.

Environmental Situation Summary for ________________ Company

Briefly summarize your areas of distinctive advantage. State what you have learned about your competition that will influence this plan. Specifically, which windows of opportunity will you seek to fill with this plan? What external factors affect this plan? What internal factors affect this plan? ____

NOTE: You will develop specific objectives and strategies for this plan in Chapters 4 and 5.

Strategy Check for Background: Your Business and Its Environment

1. After reviewing your external environment situation analysis, were you able to identify any strategic opportunities? If so, what are they? ______

______

______

______

2. After reviewing your list of your company's internal resources, list your strategies for maximizing your distinctive advantages here: ______

______

______

______

3. After studying your competition and developing strategies to address your windows of opportunity, list those strategies here: ______

______

______

______

4. Will these strategies work within the limitations you identified earlier?

EXTERNALLY LIMITING FACTORS:

Political and Legal Environment	Yes	No
Cultural and Social Environment	Yes	No
Economic Environment	Yes	No
Technological Environment	Yes	No
Competitive Environment	Yes	No
Industrial Environment	Yes	No

INTERNALLY DIRECTED FACTORS:

Goals and Objectives	Yes	No
Ethics	Yes	No
Internal Resources	Yes	No

5. What further information do you need to verify or gain in order to pursue these strategies?

______

______

______

______

4

Objectives: What Should Your Plan Do for Your Company?

Marketing objectives are specific measurement statements about what you plan to accomplish with your marketing plan. Good marketing objectives should state how you will achieve your company's stated goals; they should also contain criteria, including time limits, for measuring success and use action verbs.

Objectives should state:

What is to be achieved
When
By Whom
How will it be *measured*

The objectives of your marketing plan should support one or more of the company goals that you selected in Chapter 1. We recommend that you define maximum and minimum levels of achievement for your objectives as shown in the following example:

> **Goal:** To profitably introduce a new product to XYZ market.
>
> **Minimum marketing objective:** Sales staff educates XYZ market about the benefits of new product in three ways over the next nine months.
>
> **Maximum marketing objective:** Company fills orders from 5 percent of XYZ market for new product over the next nine months.

Often marketing planners do not have complete authority to carry out the plans developed for each objective. Therefore, it is helpful to state *who* is responsible for achieving each objective.

Importance of Company Objectives to Your Plan

It may be difficult at first to relate the objectives of your marketing plan to your company's overall vision and goals. However, tying marketing actions to the intended direction of your company helps ensure both support for your ideas and success for your projects. It can also help you choose your marketing strategy when several options are available.

Your company's management would not be spending time and money on you and your marketing plan unless it had specific ideas about what it wanted from you as the marketing expert. It is imperative that you reaffirm your company's goals with the person or group that will ultimately have to approve your plans. Having consensus on goals generates the support you need to develop strategies for meeting those goals.

Developing marketing strategies based on solidly defined objectives gives you an advantage over others. It enables you to take advantage of the windows of opportunity you identified in Chapter 3 by analyzing your internal resources and your competition.

STRATEGIC PLAYSHEET 8.

Example Setting Marketing Objectives for *La Jolla Landscaping* **Company**

Rewrite the two marketing goals for your company that you identified in Chapter 1. List a maximum and a minimum marketing objective that will move your company toward each goal.

GOAL 1 *To increase our share of the landscaping business in La Jolla*

[Each goal may require one or more specific actions. Those actions are objectives. Write both minimum and maximum objectives for goals. By setting these expectations, you will have a broader range within which to achieve success.]

OBJECTIVES	DATE	
	Minimum	Maximum
What is to be achieved?	*Introduce our company to 300 new prospective clients*	*Introduce the entire coastal area to our business via direct mailing of our brochure*
By when?	*April 1, 1993*	*April 1, 1993*
By whom?	*our sales force and our brochure*	*our brochure*
How will it be measured?	*phone inquiries & new accounts*	*increase phone inquiries & new accounts*

GOAL 2 *To become the company of choice for residential landscaping maintenance*

OBJECTIVES	DATE	
	Minimum	Maximum
What is to be achieved?	*10 new residential accounts*	*35 new residential accounts (all we can manage for now)*
By when?	*May 1, 1993*	*May 1, 1993*
By whom?	*sales staff*	*sales staff*
How will it be measured?	*actual accounts*	*actual accounts*

STRATEGIC PLAYSHEET 8.

Setting Marketing Objectives for ______________________ Company

Rewrite the two marketing goals for your company that you identified in Chapter 1. List a maximum and a minimum marketing objective that will move your company toward each goal.

GOAL 1 ____

____

[Each goal may require one or more specific actions. Those actions are objectives. Write both minimum and maximum objectives for goals. By setting these expectations, you will have a broader range within which to achieve success.]

OBJECTIVES		DATE
	Minimum	Maximum
What is to be achieved?		
By when?		
By whom?		
How will it be measured?		

GOAL 2 ____

____

____

OBJECTIVES		DATE
	Minimum	Maximum
What is to be achieved?		
By when?		
By whom?		
How will it be measured?		

Objectives: What Should Your Plan Do for Your Company?

The objectives for a marketing plan help focus your energies and resources to obtain maximum results with minimal experimentation. The objectives also help you avoid the mistakes that come with using a trial-and-error method. Good marketing plans can increase the number of successes your company experiences and reduce the amount of time and money wasted—leading to increased profits that help pay your salary!

You have defined clear, measurable objectives for your marketing plan and have a sense of both your business environment and your competition's strengths and weaknesses. Now, you are ready to consider strategies that build on that knowledge, with maximum benefit for your markets and your company.

The Adjustable Opportunities

5

Just Markets or Target Markets

With a clear view of your company and its competitive environment, and with concrete objectives for the immediate future, you are now ready to make strategic marketing decisions. The first of these decisions is the selection of your target markets—those groups that your company needs to serve in order to maintain a profit.

The difference between target marketing and everyone marketing is similar to the difference between using a rifle and aiming at a target and using a shotgun and hoping to get close enough to the target to score some points. The more precisely you select, design, and aim your products, prices, distribution, and promotions to profitable target markets, the more successful your company will be.

Company planners often make the mistake of assuming that everyone, individual and business, will want, need, and use their product or service. They also frequently overlook their present customers when predicting the market for a new product or service. In fact, your current customers are your most important target markets for additional sales and for referral business.

Not all of the businesses or consumers that are located in your service area will be in the market, that is, will want or need your product or service at any given time. Even the major soft drink manufacturers have only about half of the soft drink market. So what is a market?

Broadly, a potential market is consumers or businesses with:

- Needs and/or wants
- Money to spend
- The willingness to spend it

Using these criteria, the everyone market can be narrowed to broad segments, or groups, that have common characteristics, including common needs. Generally, the smaller the segment, the easier it is to make a mutually satisfying and profitable exchange of your products and services with that segment. However, each market segment you consider for a separate marketing plan must have three characteristics—measurability, accessibility, and profitability.

Hundreds of stories exist about successful advertising or sales campaigns for unprofitable products or services. Be sure that your product or service is profitable before you promote it!

Major Market Segments: Individual Consumers and Business Clients

All products and services can be offered to at least two major markets: individuals and businesses (or groups). Many marketing planners make the mistake of focusing on only the end user when looking for markets to target, neglecting the business markets between your company and the final consumer—the middlemen. (Middlemen are described in Chapter 8.) Effective marketing planners consider both broad segments.

You may enjoy drinking Coke or Pepsi. Both companies advertise extensively to let you know about their products. However, both companies must also market extensively to the middlemen—grocery chains, convenience stores, gas stations, fast-food restaurants—to make sure that their products are available to you. All of us individually are part of the consumer market for Coke and Pepsi; the grocery chains and other major distributors are part of the business market for Coke and Pepsi.

Strategies for Targeting Markets

Traditional Mass Markets

Mass marketing is the term for the marketing approach that gives information about a product or service with general appeal to large numbers of people. This approach is often used to promote small consumer items, such as detergents, food stuffs, and cosmetics, and large expensive items, such as automobiles and appliances. Mass marketing is usually very expensive because it promotes the product or service to many people who are not in the market for it as well as to those who are. This form of marketing may not differentiate between your business client and your end consumer. Mass marketing is profitable only if the company builds in an adequate profit margin on frequently replaced items or a larger margin on infrequently purchased items.

Single Target Markets

As marketing professionals have learned more about buyer behavior patterns and the strengths and weaknesses of their marketing promotion tools, they have been able to refine the process for identifying and targeting markets. Market identification requires grouping markets according to various demographic characteristics in order to estimate the needs of any specific group or segment. Single market identification—the ability to target a single market—is one result of this refinement. It enables planners to reach and serve each market in an efficient, direct manner.

Single target marketing works extremely well. Most companies interact with at least two market types, other businesses and end consumers. They know that changing environments make it dangerous to depend on a single market. Although in practice most companies realize the necessity of targeting more than one market, they have traditionally developed separate marketing plans for each individual market segment.

Affinity Target Markets

Marketing planners have discovered that markets reflect general trends in society. One important trend emphasizes the value of the individual with special interests and needs. Although businesses and consumers appear to be demographically similar, in reality their needs may be very diverse. This makes it difficult to target a group large enough to be profitable by relying solely on demographic segmentation.

This realization has led astute planners to group markets according to their common needs by focusing on what individual consumers and businesses need and want instead of on their demographics. It is possible to identify businesses and even specific individuals who share a need for the benefits provided by your products and services. These customers' only affinity may be their common need. Although you may use different promotion strategies to deliver your message to different markets, the message remains constant because the needs and the derived benefits are the same or very similar.

Affinity target markets are illustrated in Figure 5-1.

Selecting Your Strategies

As you read through the following parts of this chapter, select your strategies for identifying markets for your company's products and services and then narrow them

Figure 5-1. Affinity target markets.

down to one or more target markets. You may want to consider at least one business market and a group of individual consumers. Additional markets should be chosen for their potential rate of return to your company. Depending on the strategies you have chosen, your markets may be grouped either on the basis of demographics or on the basis of common needs. In either case, try to find out as much as possible about these markets and what their needs and wants are.

Target Market 1 Business ______________________

Target Market 2 Consumer ______________________

Target Market 3 Other ______________________

Target Market 4 Other ______________________

Planning Exercise 5-1.
Mass Marketing Strategy

List your product and/or service here: ______________________

____

State why you have chosen this strategy to identify your target markets. ______________________

____

____

Target Market

Planning Exercise 5-2.
Single Target Marketing Strategy

List your product and/or service here: ______________________

____

State why you have chosen this strategy to identify your target markets. ______________________

____

____

Business Markets

Consumer Markets

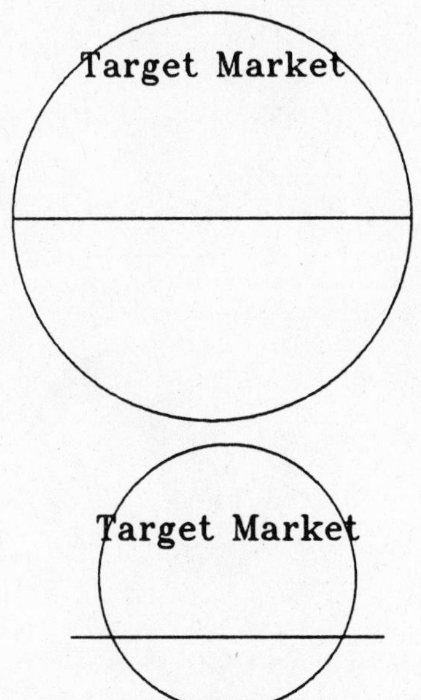

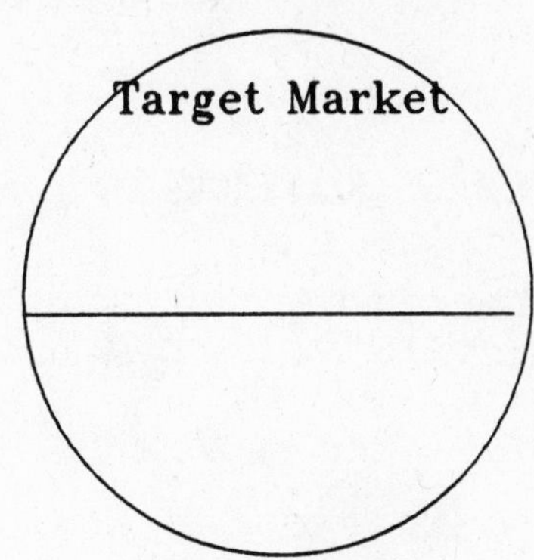

Target Market ____________________

Target Market ____________________

Planning Exercise 5-3.
Affinity Target Marketing Strategy

List your product and/or service here: ____

____

State why you have chosen this strategy to identify your target markets. ________________

____

____

The targeted areas represent the areas of overlapping needs of each type of market.

Business Markets		Consumer Markets	
Market # 1	______________	Market # 1	______________
Market # 2	______________	Market # 2	______________
Market # 3	______________	Market # 3	______________

Common Needs of BUSINESS MARKETS Will Often Overlap

Common Needs of CONSUMER MARKETS Will Often Overlap

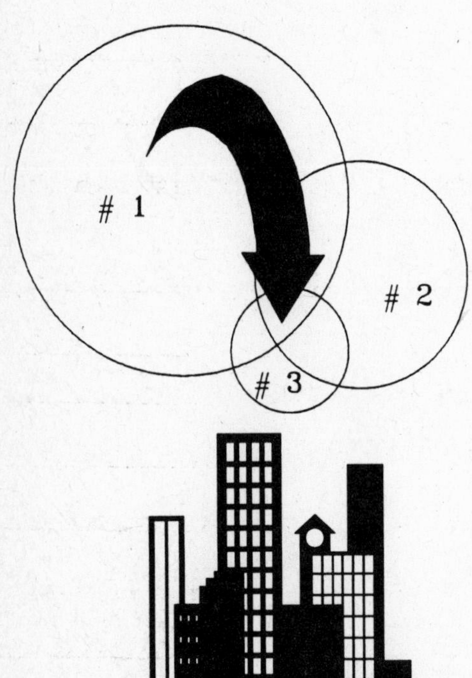

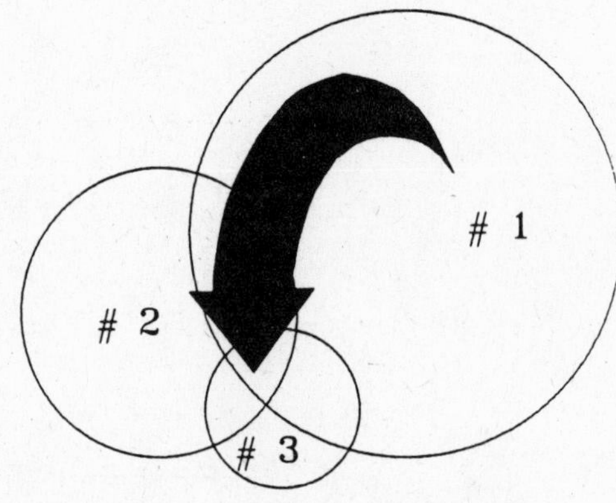

Business Markets

Consumer Markets

Describing Major Market Segments

You can never know too much about your market segments. However, most companies have limited time and financial resources available for market research. The following lists give you an idea of the kinds of information that may be important for you to know about your markets. Don't forget to include information about your current customers; they are not only one of your most important markets, they are also the most easily accessed. It is always necessary to know as much as possible about the needs and desires of any market that you are considering; this desire forms the basis for your promotion of your product or service to that market.

Planning Exercise 5-4.
Business Target Markets

IDENTIFYING BUSINESS TARGET MARKETS

Characteristics	*Market 1*	*Market 2*	*Market 3*	*Market 4*
Demographics				
Location				
local				
regional				
national				
international				
Company background				
history, age				
ownership				
types of clients				
products/services				
number of employees				
offices				
major suppliers				
landmark discoveries or legal decisions				
current trends				
Income patterns				
Sales volume				
by products				
by markets				
Major expenses				
Income and reported earnings				
Seasonality of cash flow				
Buying power				
Cash available				
Buying habits				
Current, former, or new customers				

Characteristics	Market 1	Market 2	Market 3	Market 4
Purpose of purchase				
Importance of small differences				
Kinds of buying				
new task				
modified rebuy				
straight rebuy				
Frequency of purchases				
Volume of purchases				
Timing of purchases in relation to business cycle				
Accessibility of decision maker				

Planning Exercise 5-5.
Consumer Target Markets

IDENTIFYING CONSUMER TARGET MARKETS

Characteristics	Market 1	Market 2	Market 3	Market 4
Demographics				
Age				
Sex				
Location				
region				
urban				
suburban				
rural				
Marital status				
single				
married				
mingles				
divorced				
widowed				
Family life cycle				
single				
young married				
no children				
full house				
young children				
older children				
dependent children				

Characteristics	*Market 1*	*Market 2*	*Market 3*	*Market 4*
empty nest				
no children at home				
older, single				
Education				
Occupation				
Nationality, race				
Religion				
Income patterns				
Income, actual cash				
Buying power				
money available				
Social and psychographic factors				
Life-styles				
Social groups				
Cultural values				
Shopping patterns				
Leisure activities				
Reference groups				
large (e.g., baby boomers)				
small (e.g., clubs)				
Personality type				
Attitudes, opinions				

Review the information you have compiled in Planning Exercises 5-1 through 5-5. Select one or more target markets for this plan, either business or consumer. Ask yourself the following questions before you proceed.

1. Does this market(s) appear to need or want your products?
2. Does this market(s) have the ability to return what your company needs from it?
3. Are the members able and willing to spend the money to purchase your products and services?
4. If so, would the market(s) be profitable for your company to serve?

Prioritize your markets, because a focused impact is more successful than a scattered one. Select markets in which you can measure your success in achieving the objectives outlined in Chapter 4 that are easily accessed by your company or its representatives and that are potentially profitable.

You will probably plan to approach several of the markets listed. If so, you may want to prepare a separate marketing strategy mix for each target market or affinity market cluster. These plans will be consolidated and interrelated to form your total marketing plan.

For simplicity, we suggest that you review your options with others who may share responsibility for the success of marketing planning within your company or organization. If you need more information about the markets selected, seek it. Narrow your focus to the most profitable market choice in each list, and choose one or all of those market segments to use as you work through the rest of your marketing plan.

Targeting Market Needs

After you have identified as many facts as you can about your possible markets or have decided to use the affinity targeting strategy, decide:

- What do you know that your market wants and/or needs from your company?
- What does your company want and need from these markets?

Then identify the characteristics of your markets. Can a mutually satisfying exchange be made with this market or markets? Will your products and services solve its wants, needs, and problems at an acceptable profit and within the objectives you have chosen? Check your measurable objectives to see if these markets are acceptable.

STRATEGIC PLAYSHEET 9.

Example Description of Target Markets by Facts and Needs

If you think a target market wants or needs your products and services, re-analyze the actual needs of that market(s) here.

DESCRIPTION OF TARGET MARKET

Target Market Name: *Local Affluent Zip Code*

Description of Facts	Description of Needs
upscale Indianapolis area	*Services:*
houses $300,000 to $500,000	*cleaning*
3 + cars per household	*yard care*
50% of households have double income	*child care day and/or night*
2 children per household 0 to 17 yrs.	*Products:*
homeowners ages 35 to 50	*upscale appliances*
	toys
	executive toys—boats, expensive cars
	Social:
	recognition
	cause to support

If you can't find a "need" match to your company, either change markets or modify products, whichever is cheaper. Selection of the appropriate target market(s) is the most important adjustable factor in your marketing strategy mix. Identifying their NEEDS correctly is the second most important task in marketing planning.

STRATEGIC PLAYSHEET 9.

Description of Target Markets by Facts and Needs

If you think a target market wants or needs your products and services, re-analyze the actual needs of that market(s) here.

DESCRIPTION OF TARGET MARKET

Target Market Name: ______________________________

Description of Facts	Description of Needs

If you can't find a "need" match to your company, either change markets or modify products, whichever is cheaper. Selection of the appropriate target market(s) is the most important adjustable factor in your marketing strategy mix. Identifying their NEEDS correctly is the second most important task in marketing planning.

Strategy Check for Target Market(s) Selected

1. Name your target market(s). ______________________________

____

____

____

____

2. What is your strategy reasoning (based on above analysis)? ______________________________

____

____

____

____

____

____

3. Will your strategy work within the parameters you identified earlier?

EXTERNALLY LIMITING FACTORS		
Political and legal environment	Yes	No
Cultural and social environment	Yes	No
Economic environment	Yes	No
Technological environment	Yes	No
Competitive environment	Yes	No
Industrial environment	Yes	No
INTERNALLY DIRECTED FACTORS:		
Goals and objectives	Yes	No
Ethics	Yes	No
Internal resources	Yes	No

4. State the objective this strategy will help to fulfill. ______________________________

____

____

6

Product-Service Mix

At this point you have considered the definition of marketing as a process, and you have learned the importance of focusing on your markets, not just in a broad sense but with tools and theories with which to segment those markets into more desirable target markets. The more you know about each target market's needs and desires, the better are your chances of serving that market to your mutual satisfaction. In this and the next three chapters, we focus on those adjustable elements of the marketing plan that you can directly control—the 4 Ps. The first P is the product-service mix.

Product-Service Mix: A Definition

In the marketing sense, a product-service mix is the total grouping of tangible and intangible attributes your company offers to satisfy your customer's and target market's needs, wants, and desires. It is important that you know and understand exactly what it is that these markets want to buy so that you may offer it to them. As the saying goes, cosmetic companies don't sell lipstick, they sell hope—and it comes in many colors! Many companies show you how to apply that hope right there in the store where it is sold. This added service is a good example of a product-service mix.

Remember that while you may view your products in terms of their physical attributes, your customers buy the benefits or perceived value of your products and services—the total of your product-service mix. For example, consider a very successful car dealership that claims to offer an exciting mode of transportation that is both affordable and desirable. A well-trained, amicable sales force able to offer low-cost financing to a large portion of the population increases the perceived value of the dealership and helps assure success in selling its product-service mix to its target market.

Services can be marketed just like products; however, services are usually tied to the reputation and image of the service provider. For instance, although the service offered at the local barbershop is haircutting, in reality the service rendered may also include listening and advice. The service provider is the key to the customer's perception of valuable service gained. Companies use a combination of products and services to enhance the perceived value of their offerings.

A simple rule of thumb is:

To enhance tangible products, add services.
To enhance intangible services, add products.

Components of Product-Service Mix

Physical Attributes

The physical, tangible product and the explainable, intangible services are usually the basis for any product-service mix. The company owners may have begun with a plan to make something (skis, bookcases, butterfly nets), or they may have decided to offer a service (research reports, interior design, tax return preparation). Before promoting or offering products and services to your target markets, you and everyone else involved in the marketing process of your company should be keenly aware of exactly what your product is.

Quality

Quality is an expected degree of excellence consistent with your company's image and the characteristics of the products you offer. Quality seems to be identifiable only when a product fails to live up to the customer's expectation. Although not all products are expected to last forever, all products do have a minimum performance expectation. There is nothing more irritating to a buyer than purchasing a product or service that does not fully meet expectations.

You need to acknowledge your target market's expectations for your product's performance and longevity and then promote those product characteristics that satisfy your market's need for quality. This point is particularly important when you are introducing a new product to complement an existing one or to extend your product line. The degree of excellence set by the first product should be adhered to for the rest of the product line. If the new product or service becomes less desirable or is perceived as having less quality, it may destroy the reputation of the entire product line you've developed.

Company and Brand Identification

Once your company has established itself as an entity, it begins to develop a company image or identity through its selection of a name, its manner of operations, and its reputation for dealing with customers. Because you have already selected a target market, you can mold your company image to fit the needs and expectations of that market.

As a company gets larger, it extends and reinforces its good image through branding. Just as the cattlemen branded their herds, so do companies brand their products and services. Your brand or image quickly conveys the type and quality of your products and services to your markets.

By the time you introduce additional products to complement an existing product, you will have developed brand recognition for your products. This gives you the advantage of using the success of the first product and services to introduce the second, the first and second to introduce the third, and so on. This should stimulate sales of your previous products, because the promotions from the new products and services reinforce information about your previous ones.

Packaging

Packaging refers to the way your products and services are presented to your target markets. The package serves three useful purposes:

- Protecting the product
- Educating consumers about the quality and uses of the product
- Promoting the product and company identity

Packaging can and should reflect the tastes and desires of your market and may be modified to appeal to different markets at different times and places. The package may be your only opportunity to sell your product so it has to speak for itself. Packaging is more than mere labelling; it also includes positioning your product and appealing to the proper segment of your market with the right message.

A company that offers predominantly services, such as medical, legal, accounting, and other technical skills, may still achieve benefits from packaging of services. The service package reinforces the image of the service provider through consistent use of the company name and its symbol or logo on everything from name tags in the reception area to report covers and billing statements.

Added Services

Although service can be the product itself, it can also significantly enhance a product. As society becomes more and more dependent on services offered by a variety of people, customers expect services in addition to basic products. Some services that add benefits and increase the perceived value of your products to your markets include:

- Follow-up after the sale
- Guarantees and warranties
- Pick-up and delivery
- Training
- Counseling
- Storage
- Coordination
- Networking
- Advance notice of sales, new products, special promotions

Increasing the services offered with your products also increases your costs. (Factoring these increased costs into your pricing is discussed in Chapter 7.) If your market is sensitive to price adjustments, it may not be appropriate to add services.

Planning Exercise 6-1.
Your Product-Service Mix

The following list may help to describe your product-service mix:

Product

Does your company offer predominantly tangible products? ______

Are your products new or old standards? ______

Are your products improved versions of familiar items or are they unique? ______

How many lines (types of items) do you offer? ______

What is the quality of each (or the quality range)? ______

______

How are your products packaged? ______

Is safety a factor? ______

Does the packaging need to educate? ______

Does it consistently promote your image? ______

Do you carry name brands, your own brands, or a combination?

______

Service

Is your company a strictly service business? ______

What services do you offer? ______

How do you describe your services? ______

What is the quality range of your services? ______

How are your services packaged? ______

Is safety or confidentiality a factor? ______

Does the packaging need to educate or explain? ______

Does it consistently promote your image? ______

Mix

Does your company offer a mix of products and services? ______

If so, which is predominant—product or service? ______

What additional services do you offer (for example, training, delivery, counseling, storage, coordination)? ______

______

______

After completing Planning Exercise 6-1, complete Planning Exercise 6-2 to summarize your product-service mix characteristics.

Planning Exercise 6-2.
Product-Service Mix Characteristics

PRODUCT-SERVICE MIX CHARACTERISTICS SUMMARY

Physical Attributes	Quality	Company & Brand Image	Packaging	Added Services
Services				
Products				

Features and Facts vs. Benefits and Uses

The profits your company earns by offering products and services for sale keep the business operating and enable it to offer more products and services to existing and future clients. As a business planner, you need to know your products' features and strengths. Remember, however, that your clients and customers do not purchase those features; they purchase the perceived value of what your products and services can do for them (see Figure 6-1). The only way to determine which benefits are important is to match your products' features to the needs of your selected markets.

Features define the facts about your product or service. They tell you if your

Figure 6-1. Perceptions of your total product.

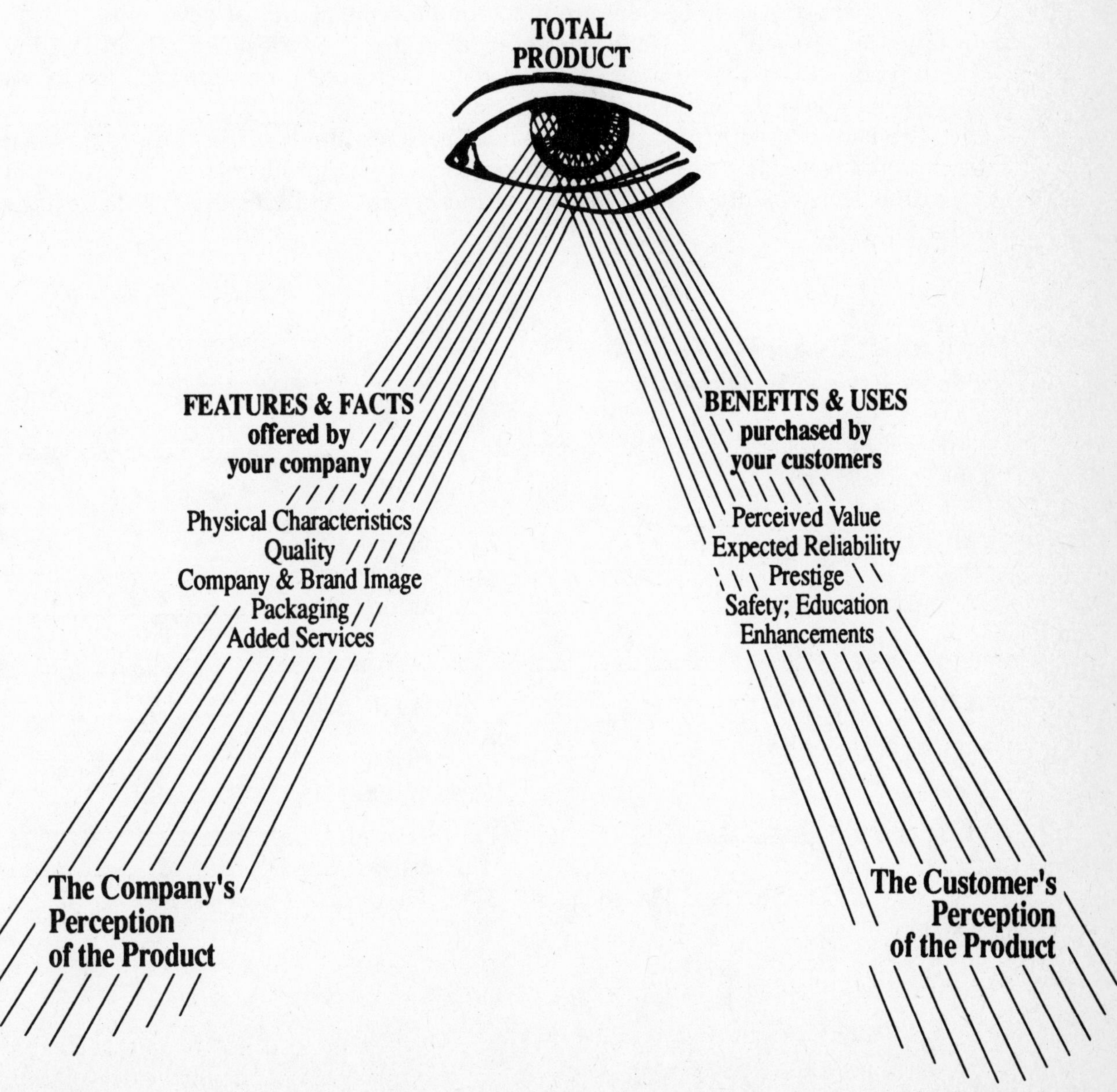

product is big or small, light or dark, available night or day, and so on. When you describe your product or service factually, you are telling your customer about the features of your products.

However, benefits are what make your customers want to purchase your products and services. A benefit answers questions such as, "What can this product or service do for me?" and "Why would I like to purchase this product or service?" The most successful marketing executives have learned to "show, tell, and sell"—promoting the benefits of their products and services and backing up those benefits with features or facts. For example, the color red may be a feature of your product, but this feature may mean different things to different markets. For some, the important benefit of the color red may be that it is easily seen and helps promote safety; for others, red may be a school color that arouses fond recollections of school days, while for a bank officer, red may mean debts, as "in the red," and may therefore evoke an undesirable image.

If you are developing a new product, you have the luxury of developing it to fit your target market's needs exactly. However, even if you are dealing with an existing product, you may be able to modify it to satisfy the market's needs or to identify an existing benefit that the market will appreciate.

The list of benefits to the target market becomes the focus of the promotional information directed to that market. Once you look at your products and services from your market's viewpoint, you will find numerous benefits and uses that will be of value to your markets.

Planning Exercise 6-3.
Product-Service Mix Perceptions

Complete the following exercise. Use the product-service and target market you have selected for this marketing plan.

FEATURES & FACTS offered by your company ______	BENEFITS & USES purchased by your customers ______
Physical Characteristics ______	Perceived Value ______
Quality ______	Expected Reliability ______
Company & Brand Image ______	Prestige ______
Packaging ______	Safety; Education ______
Added Services ______	Enhancements ______

Now fill in Strategic Playsheet 10, Matching Product-Service Mix to Target Markets.

STRATEGIC PLAYSHEET 10.

Example Matching Product-Service Mix to Target Markets

MARKETING OBJECTIVE *to increase number of estate planning clients by 10% before end of year*

TARGET MARKET *retired professional men and women*

COMPANY'S PERCEPTION OF PRODUCT OR SERVICE

Target Market Description	Product-Service Features
60 + men and women	*asset review*
residents of retirement	*preparation of wills &*
community	*trusts*
	office located nearby
	CPAs & attorneys on
	staff

CUSTOMER'S PERCEPTION OF PRODUCT OR SERVICE

Target Market Needs	Product-Service Benefits
protection from unethical	*long standing good*
practices and people	*reputation of firm*
estate planning	*specialists in field of*
	estate planning

STRATEGIC PLAYSHEET 10.

Matching Product-Service Mix to Target Markets

MARKETING OBJECTIVE ____________________

____

TARGET MARKET ____________________

COMPANY'S PERCEPTION OF PRODUCT OR SERVICE

Target Market Description	Product-Service Features
________________	________________
________________	________________
________________	________________
________________	________________
________________	________________
________________	________________

CUSTOMER'S PERCEPTION OF PRODUCT OR SERVICE

Target Market Needs	Product-Service Benefits
________________	________________
________________	________________
________________	________________
________________	________________
________________	________________
________________	________________

The Product Life Cycle

Products, like people, go through different stages of life. The concept of the product life cycle can be applied to industries and loosely applied to an individual company for purposes of considering possible strategies:

- For *new* or *developing* products and services, sales increase but profits are low because of the high cost of penetrating the market.
- For *growing* products and services, sales climb rapidly, and profits start to rise.
- During the *maturing* stage, sales start to taper off, and profits may drop due to increased competition.
- In the *declining* phase, both sales and profits decrease. Declining products and services need special care during the phase-out period. Markets want "new and improved" products and services, but they tend to want to be gently eased out of the old way and into the new one. This process, called demarketing, requires planning to ease out unprofitable products and services without losing your markets to competitors.

Successful businesses use a visual and numerical approach to balance their product mixes so that newer products can be financed by the more established, profitable products. Newer products can often enhance and extend the life of older, possibly declining products.

Planning Exercise 6-4.
Product-Service Life Cycle

List your major products or services under the column that you believe describes each product or service. Then look at your sales records for each product and service you have listed. Place an X for each product or service at the appropriate point on the activity curve (see example below).

PRODUCT-SERVICE LIFE CYCLE FOR ______________________ COMPANY

Example

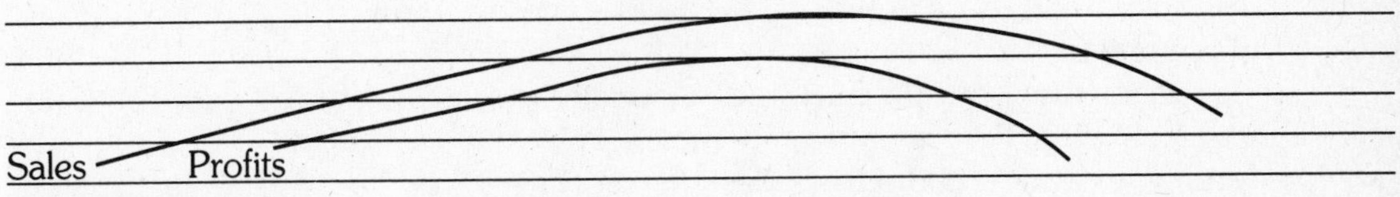

Sales Profits

New/Developing Growing Maturing Declining

1.
2.
3.
4.
5.

PRODUCT-SERVICE LIFE CYCLE FOR ______________________ COMPANY

____

____

____

____

____

New/Developing	Growing	Maturing	Declining

1.
2.
3.
4.
5.

From this list and the graph, evaluate how well your product mix works for your company. Are your products and services in all phases of the product life cycle? Or are your products and services concentrated in one or two phases?

Name the product-service for which you are developing this plan: ______________

In what phase of the product life cycle is it located? ______________________

Options for Your Product-Service Mix

After you have matched your current product-service mix to your market's needs and identified where your products and services lie on the product life cycle curve, you can explore other product mix options. There are a number of strategies you might use, depending on your company's goals:

- Remain steady—continue with current mix.
- Expand—add more products or services, related or unrelated.
- Trade up—add more expensive products to your offerings.
- Trade down—add less expensive products to your lines.
- Contract—trim your product line, especially products with low profit margins and for which there is reduced demand.
- Modify existing products—redesign, repackage, update image for a fresh approach, or introduce new and improved versions of your products.
- Position products—reposition your products relative to your competitors' products. Where can you take advantage of windows of opportunity by using your distinctive advantage?

The last two options are tricky, but are worth considering to increase profits. The risk is that, if you move out of the perceived value range of your products and services, you may lose your current markets.

Strategy Check for Product-Service Mix Selected

1. Name your target markets: ______________________________

____

____

____

2. Based on your analysis, what is your product-service strategy to serve these markets? ____

____

____

____

3. Will this strategy work within the limitations you identified earlier?

EXTERNALLY LIMITING FACTORS:

Political and legal environment	Yes	No
Cultural and social environment	Yes	No
Economic environment	Yes	No
Technological environment	Yes	No
Competitive environment	Yes	No
Industrial environment	Yes	No

INTERNALLY DIRECTED FACTORS:

Goals and objectives	Yes	No
Ethics	Yes	No
Internal resources	Yes	No

4. State the objective this strategy will help to fulfill. ______________________________

____

____

____

7

The Right Pricing Mix

Prices are important in our economy because they directly influence the allocation of resources—yours, your suppliers', and your customers'. In the marketing planning process, price is the measure of exchange; often, it determines whether the exchange between the target markets and your company will be made at all and whether it will be profitable.

Price is the total your target market pays to receive the benefits or uses of your products or services. It includes money, time, and, possibly, risk, as well as any fees, extra expenses, and implicit costs, for example, hotel and transportation expenses to attend a three-day seminar.

Pricing is determined by many factors. The following examples show some of the frustrations of setting prices and point out some of the marketing opportunities available when you look at your pricing policy as an integral part of your marketing plan.

What would you pay for a ballpoint pen? In 1945, when the ballpoint pen was first introduced, a New York department store priced it at $12.50—and sold 10,000 before the end of the first day.

Consider the price of airfare from Denver to New York. The price might range from nothing to $25 for a child under 2 years old, for the crew, or for a parcel. However, the price may be $300 at nonpeak travel times, during competitive price wars, through travel agency packages or for seniors—or it might be $2,000 or more for private jet service.

Ideally, you would like the prices of your products and services to reflect a good balance between their perceived value to your customers and the needs of your company to cover costs and maintain a profit. If this were always possible, the prices you charge would be based on the needs and willingness of your markets to purchase, and your costs and the profits necessary to maintain a healthy business. However, factors dictated by the external environment of your company and by your company's internal environment also affect your pricing decisions and strategies.

General Pricing Strategies

Determining price in the marketing sense depends on three factors:

- The target markets and their demand for the product or service
- The company's objectives, resources, and ethics
- The external environment, including competition

As you determine prices for your products or services, you will consciously or unconsciously develop a pricing strategy for your company. Each time a company sets a price, it runs the risks of pricing products and services too high to meet the customers' needs or too low to meet the company's profit goals.

Two widely used general pricing strategies are *skim-the-cream* and *penetration* pricing. Skim-the-cream pricing strategy gets its name from an old term for taking the rich cream off of the top of the milk. It means much the same thing in pricing policies: charging higher initial prices for products or services that appeal to the top of the markets and then reducing prices over time as the company seeks broader markets. Penetration pricing strategy, in contrast, sets prices in the low (but still profitable) range and offers products and services through a wide variety or large number of distribution channels to a large number of markets.

In this chapter, you will set parameters to help determine your pricing strategies. You will look at environmental factors that are external to your company and internal company factors that influence your pricing decisions. You will determine your costs and figure what it takes for your company to break even in order to establish a profit structure. Once you know your break-even point, you can adopt strategies to meet your objectives.

Externally Dictated Factors

In the real business world, it is seldom possible to consider only the market's needs and your profits. You must also weigh the effects of the externally dictated factors discussed in Chapter 3. Let's look at each of these factors and briefly review its possible impact on your pricing decisions.

- *Political and Legal Environment.* Price decisions are highly regulated, particularly for interstate trade. Over the years, laws have been enacted to encourage competition and to protect small businesses and consumers from potentially unethical practices. In addition, states and cities have licensing fees and sales tax requirements for many types of businesses and products or services.
- *Cultural and Social Environment.* At first glance, this factor may not seem to affect your pricing decisions. However, in many industries, pricing strategies have been influenced by cultural and social factors. If they affect your industry, you are probably familiar with these and other examples:
    - *Expected price.* Expected price is related to the customers' perceived value of the benefits of your products and services and is often based on the price of similar items or services. This trend bears monitoring because it affects profit margins at every price level.
    - *Price lining.* Prices of all products or services are categorized within a few price levels, e.g., moderately priced, better dresses, and designer labels; amateur or professional fees; gifts under $10, under $20, under $50.
    - *Prestige pricing.* Higher prices are charged for items with status or exceptional quality.
    - *Odd amounts.* Items are often priced at uneven amounts, e.g. $4.95 or $97.99, in the belief that pricing just under the expected top of the price ranges has a

psychological advantage. Such pricing is often used in grocery and other retail settings.

- *Economic Environment.* This factor affects prices in two areas: (1) the economy of the country, region, and city and its influence on your markets' ability to purchase, and (2) the demand/supply factors of your industry, which determine elasticity, or the way demand reacts to price changes. If demand (quantity of sales) increases as prices decrease, it is elastic. If demand (quantity of sales) remains relatively constant as prices increase (or decrease), it is inelastic; this is the case for products or services, such as specialized computer parts for industry and dialysis machines for patients with kidney diseases, that are absolutely required by the market. Similarly, if higher prices increase supplies, supply is elastic; if higher prices do not bring substantial increases in supply, supply is inelastic.
- *Technological Environment.* As new technology increases or decreases your production, service, distribution, and/or promotion costs, there will be a direct impact on your pricing options. Sometimes, the expectation of new or improved technologies may encourage customers and potential customers to postpone their purchases.
- *Competitive Environment.* As you analyzed your competition in Chapter 3, you identified windows of opportunity—areas where your company enjoys a unique advantage. Competition is a major factor in your pricing decisions. It is especially important to identify the following about your competitors when you set prices on new products or services or when you adjust your current prices.

  - Is there a company or firm that sets the pricing standards in your industry? Where do your company's prices fall in relation to those of the price leader?
  - Are there standard prices—hourly rates, delivery costs, project costs? It is important to know what is considered the norm among your competitors.
  - What are your actions and reactions to your competitors' pricing policies? Do you ignore them, meet or beat their prices, try rebates or coupons, or adjust your discount schedules? You might also try competing on a nonprice basis, by offering nonprice incentives such as increased services, warranties, premiums, or free samples.

- *Industrial Environment.* The industrial environment has developed two conflicting trends in recent years: (1) the move toward cooperation within industries, and (2) the trend toward fierce competition within the industry. You should identify which trend your industry tends to follow because this environment sets the stage for most of your marketing planning decisions. Whatever your business, many of your market's expectations about conducting business with you are based on the general image of your industry, its policies and general ethics.

Internally Directed Factors

Internally directed factors, as discussed in Chapter 3, are those that form the company environment within which your marketing planning develops, is budgeted for, and is implemented. These factors are important in your pricing decisions in the following areas:

▪ *Company Goals and Objectives* determine where your company's management wants to be and therefore the focus of your marketing plan and its pricing strategies. Because goals vary from company to company, marketing plans that have worked for other companies may not be appropriate to yours at this time. Four major corporate goals that influence pricing decisions are:

- Profit orientation. This includes companies that set target rates of return on investment or on net sales, as well as those that set profit maximization goals. If the major goals are income and profit, you need to work with the financial managers to develop plans which will increase prices, decrease expenses, or, more likely, both. If your marketing budget is not income/profit-oriented, your plans may not be funded.
- Sales orientation. These companies set goals for increasing sales or improving market share. You may have to encourage management to blend sales and profit objectives.
- Status quo. Companies that follow strong price leaders tend to support plans that will maintain their company's position in relation to the price leader. The basic objective is stability. In the current competitive environment, this objective may not be possible for the long term.
- Survival. As the external environment puts more pressure on businesses, survival in the short-run (until the economy improves) may be the corporate objective determining your pricing decisions as well as your marketing budgets.

▪ *Corporate Ethics* should define codes of conduct within the company as well as outside. The ethical environment of your company may enhance or may limit what you are able to do with your marketing plans as well as what you may do personally.

▪ *Internal Resources*—capacity, equipment, inventory, manpower, and money—may be limited in the short term. Within these resources, you will be expected to develop and implement pricing strategies that make the best use of the company's resources and provide profits for continued development. Your variables may include suggested prices, discounts, and allowances. (These will be discussed later in this chapter.) Plans for marketing your products may also be in direct competition for resources and budget approval internally.

Cost and Profit Factors in Pricing Strategies

Your costs provide a floor for your pricing decisions, while your desired profits push at the ceiling of your pricing structure. Each company within each industry must make the pricing decisions that are right for it. However, two general methods of calculating prices—the cost/plus pricing method and the competitive market pricing method—provide the range of extremes. Because your pricing decisions are affected by external and internal environmental factors and by your product-service, distribution, and promotion mixes, your prices will probably fall within the range set by these two methods (see Figure 7-1).

Figure 7-1. Pricing calculation extremes.

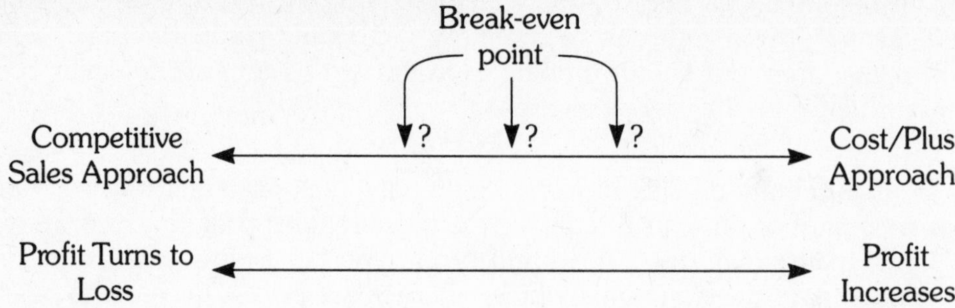

Cost/Plus Pricing

Many companies, particularly retailers, use the cost/plus approach to setting prices. They calculate what it costs them to offer the products and services and add on a predetermined percentage for profit.

$$\text{Total Costs} \times \text{Fixed \%} = \text{Price}$$

Cost/plus pricing tries to ensure a profit to the company, but it neglects the needs of the target market. Because market adjustments are made by using sales and discounts, this system is not as straightforward as it first appears. Cost/plus pricing is a totally profit-oriented approach, implemented and measured by using cost data to develop expected rates of return on the company's investment in a particular product. In a service business, costs are not an adequate base for determining profit objectives. For an example using cost/plus pricing, refer to the discussion of Wicker Industries at the end of this chapter.

Competitive Market Pricing

At the other extreme are companies that base their prices on what they think the market will pay in the current competitive environment. This strategy is called the competitive market pricing approach. Careful research on the markets and the competition is a must for businesses using this pricing strategy. It generally satisfies the needs of the customers, but companies must take care to ensure that they satisfy the need to make a profit. Many service providers use some form of this pricing strategy.

Competitive market pricing is usually determined and measured by sales data and percentage of market share. Because goals are sales-oriented (for example, to increase sales by a given percent or to establish, maintain, or increase market share), you need to be able to estimate your company's market share for each product line or service you sell. To do this, review and update your list of competitors (see Chapter 3), check the most recent total sales figures for each competitor (by units or dollars sold), add all the total sales figures, including yours, to find the total sales for your immediate market, and divide your company's total sales by the total sales of your immediate market. For example, ski industry trade associations track sales information from resorts by the numbers of skiers per day and per season. If you want to determine your resort's market share for the season, divide the number of skiers for the season at your resort by the industry's total skiers for the season. This calculation yields the percentage that is your market share.

Total Competitors Sales + Your Sales = Total Sales of Your Market

Your Sales ÷ Total Sales of Your Market = Your % Market Share

Planning Exercise 7-1.
Extreme Ranges of Prices

To determine a possible range for setting your prices, complete the following information.

1. Figure your prices based on the cost/plus method.

   What are your costs per item or unit? $________

   What rate of return do you need? times % ____X %

   Price per unit = $

2. Figure your prices based on the competitive market method.

   What is the competition charging for similar products or services? $________

   What does your research indicate that your target market is willing to pay for your products or services? $________

   Compare the two and set Price per unit = $________

These two prices give you an approximate range within which to price your product or service.

Break-Even Price

The price that covers your expenses for producing and marketing a product or service is called your break-even price.

Total Costs ÷ Total Units = Break-Even Price

The break-even price covers only costs; in order to make a profit, you need to sell your products and services at a price above break-even. It is rarely a good decision to price your products and services below your break-even level—no matter how many you sell (see Tables 7-1 and 7-2).

Table 7-1. Calculating break-even price example (given a target number of sales).

Fixed costs		$ 2,500
Variable costs:		
Selling costs (commissions, etc.) ($4.00 × 1,000 units)	$4,000	
Production costs (materials, etc.) ($3.20 × 1,000 units)	3,200	
Total variable costs		$ 7,200
TOTAL COSTS		$ 9,700
Divided by number of units		÷ 1,000 units
BREAK-EVEN PRICE		$ 9.70

Table 7-2. Calculating break-even units example (given a target price per unit).

Retail price		$9.95
Variable costs (per unit):		
Selling costs (commissions, etc.)	$ 4.00	
Production costs (materials, etc.)	3.20	
Total variable costs (per unit)		$7.20
Margin (price minus total variable costs)		$2.75
Fixed costs	$ 2,500	
Divided by margin	÷ 2.75	
BREAK-EVEN NUMBER OF UNITS		909 units

Planning Exercise 7-2.
Break-Even Pricing

To calculate your break-even price, you need to know:

1. Approximately how many units can you sell over a specified period of time (usually six months or a year)? #________

2. What are your fixed costs for that same period? $________

[Fixed costs include all of the costs your company incurs without regard to the volume of production or sales. Typically, fixed costs include advertising, rent/leasing, licenses, interest, administrative personnel costs, equipment, insurance, and utilities.]

3. What are your variable costs for the same period? ________

[Variable costs include all of the costs that vary directly with each unit produced and/or sold. If you do not produce or sell anything, your variable costs are zero. Typically, variable costs include materials, production labor, packaging, sales costs, commissions, delivery costs, and others based on your particular company needs.]

4. Add fixed costs and variable costs to figure total costs.

Fixed Costs	$
Variable Costs	+
Total Costs	$

5. Divide total costs by total units produced and/or sold over the given time period to determine your break-even price.

Total Costs ÷ Total Units = Break-Even Price

If you have an established sales price or want to calculate how many units you need to sell at various sales prices in order to break even, you can use the same cost information. (See examples on previous pages.)

Prices and Adjustments

Suggested Retail Prices

Suggested retail prices are the prices charged to the ultimate consumer of your products and some services. Many producing companies suggest retail prices for their goods based on costs, research on what the market is willing to pay, and distribution channel costs. Even if you are not currently distributing your products through a wholesaler or other distributor, your suggested retail price needs to be high enough to allow for a 50 to 60 percent discount for alternative distribution channel choices in the future. See the Wicker Industries example at the end of this chapter.

Wholesale Prices

Wholesale prices are the prices you charge to those accounts that wholesale, i.e., buy and resell and/or distribute, your products to other markets. Wholesalers provide valuable services for your company and for your ultimate consumers (see Chapter 8). Wholesalers or other distributors cover the costs of distributing your products to other markets by requiring that you give them various discounts from suggested retail prices. Then they charge the next link in the channel a marked-up percentage for their services. Obviously, the longer the channel of distribution, the higher the suggested retail price must be to pay for each wholesaler's or other distributor's services.

Planning Exercise 7-3.
Analysis of Wholesale Price Alternatives

If your company uses wholesalers or other distributors or plans to do so, analyze possible effects of various WHOLESALE DISCOUNT ALTERNATIVES for three of your products or product lines here.

WHOLESALE PRICE ALTERNATIVES (Date ________)

Products:	Suggested Retail	Amount Realized* After Wholesale Discount† of 50%	60%	Actual Company Costs
1.	$	$	$	$ ....
2.	$	$	$	$ ....
3.	$	$	$	$ ....

*Option for work sheet only
†Select discount percents that reflect your distribution needs or your typical industry standard discounts.

Adjustments to Prices

Pricing decisions affect the entire profit picture of your company. You cannot stay in business by listing prices below costs or even at the break-even point. However, your basic marketing strategies may require adjustments to price in two areas: setting discount policies and offering temporary reductions in price for existing or new products or services.

Discount Policies

Discount policies are generally built into your price structure, along with criteria for different discount options. The discount policies of your company are often the critical selling point for wholesale accounts. The profit margin must be closely monitored by both the marketing manager and the financial manager to ensure that products and services are not sold at a loss.

The example of a discount schedule in Figure 7-2 for two types of toys in a product line demonstrates both quantity and payment discounts. No allowance is given for shipping in this example. Any price changes resulting from marketing decisions, e.g., efforts to attract more wholesalers, to strengthen relationships with current wholesalers, or to encourage wholesalers to give price breaks to retailers, may require a marketing plan to implement the changes.

Factors beyond the basic price of your company's goods and services affect consumers' decisions whether to buy. Ideally, you should be able to balance the prices of your products with the products' perceived value to your customers. However, in

Figure 7-2. Wholesale price list, 1993.

QUANTITY DISCOUNT

Wholesale Discount:		TOY A	TOY B
Suggested Retail		$34.95	$6.95
6 to 24 units	40%	20.97	4.17
25 to 48 units	45%	19.22	3.82
49 to 108 units	50%	17.48	3.48
109 units and over	52%	16.78	3.34

PAYMENT DISCOUNT

Terms: Net 30 days (shipping and handling added to invoice)

practice this is seldom a perfect equation. A perceived value that is greater than price increases sales; a perceived value that is less than price decreases sales.

A company may use discounts and allowances as one method for maintaining a satisfactory price level while being able to adjust prices for certain target markets. Discounts and allowances can be temporary adjustments to price. They are used when costs for serving a given market are less than average; when a company needs to meet competitors' prices; and when it needs to reduce inventory.

Temporary Reductions

Temporary adjustments to price are the second major area in which marketing decisions affect price. Sometimes they are included in the promotion strategies. However, these pricing considerations often require financial management and marketing management to agree on strategy. Temporary adjustments to prices may include offering or changing any of the following: coupons, introductory or anniversary offers, seasonal sales, temporary raises, free or discounted services, meeting competitive actions, and negotiations and bargaining.

Planning Exercise 7-4.
Discount Factors

Consider these questions about your prices and their relation to your target markets.

What is your suggested retail price for your product-service mix? ____________________

If several products or services are offered to the target markets, what is the price range (low or high)? ____________________

If you use a wholesaler or other distributor, what is your wholesale percentage discount? ________% For what minimum quantity? ________ units (cases, carloads, etc.)

Check the discounts that you traditionally offer and those you plan to offer to your target markets, business or consumer.

	Currently Offer	Intend to Offer
Quantity purchases	________	________
Seasonal purchases	________	________
Advertising allowances	________	________
Transportation allowances	________	________
Returned goods policies	________	________
Trade-ins	________	________
Rebates	________	________
Coupons	________	________
Professional courtesy	________	________
Other	________	________

Do you offer credit? ________

If so, do you carry the credit yourself? ________

What do you charge for credit? ________

Do you accept MasterCard, Visa, or other credit cards? ________
If you do use credit cards, don't forget that the percentage the vendors charge you as the merchant is an additional cost.

Who pays for the transportation and shipping? ________

Do you offer grants or loans to qualified customers? ________

What are your other costs of extending service to this market? Explain ________

A Pricing Example: Wicker Industries

Wicker Industries' Background

Wicker Industries (a fictitious company) produces high-quality picnic baskets at three different prices. A start-up company with four employees, Wicker is owned by an engineer who works for a large oil company and who hopes to retire from the oil company in three years after building this business. Wicker, located in a small manufacturing park on the edge of town, distributes in a tri-state area. The baskets are designed for tailgate picnics and come sized to serve two, four, or eight persons. Each basket is made of sturdy reeds fitted with belt leather hinges, handles, and dividers. The basic basket contains quality dishes, glassware, and flatware. Brightly colored linen napkins and tablecloths are also included. A hot/cold vacuum bottle and storage dishes complete the set.

The Markets

Wholesale Accounts

Wicker Industries' target markets have been wholesale sales to retail stores (quality leather shops, small resort specialty shops, gourmet shops, and distinctive gift stores) and to one exclusive catalog. These accounts distribute and promote the baskets.

Direct Retail (Consumer) Accounts

Wicker has also had some success selling directly to consumers through Rolls-Royce Clubs and Mercedes Clubs, sports booster clubs, and walk-in sales at the manufacturing plant. Each group of target markets requires a differently priced product, for example, the club members were offered a slightly reduced price because the clubs assisted in promoting the baskets to their members.

Wicker Industries' Actual Costs

Wicker Industries knows that the actual cost (including fixed* and current variable costs†) per basket is:

Total Actual Costs

2-person basic basket = $ 40
4-person basic basket = $ 75
8-person deluxe basket = $145

*Fixed costs include rent, office furniture, utilities, advertising, salaries and benefits, company insurance, and certain licenses.
†Variable costs include materials and part-time labor to assemble baskets, packing, shipping, and delivery.

1993 Annual Production and Associated Costs.

	2-person basket	4-person basket	8-person basket	TOTALS
Annual production (in units*)	2,000	750	300	3,050
Annual fixed cost†	$17,000	$17,000	$17,000	$ 51,000
Annual variable costs	$63,000	$39,250	$26,500	$128,750
Break-even price per basket	$ 40	$ 75	$ 145	

*Units produced reflect an elastic demand
†Arbitrarily assigned to each product

Wholesale Prices

Wicker Industries has used the cost/plus 20 percent method to determine prices to its wholesale accounts.

Price to retailers = cost plus 20 percent

2-person basic basket = $ 48
4-person basic basket = $ 90
8-person deluxe basket = $174

Suggested Retail Prices

The retail shops marked up the baskets by approximately 100 percent (base price plus base price again).

2-person basic basket = $ 95 suggested retail price
4-person basic basket = $180 suggested retail price
8-person deluxe basket = $350 suggested retail price

The Opportunity

Wicker Industries has an opportunity to sell its premium picnic baskets through a regional distributor. However, in order to do so, it must be able to sell baskets to the regional distributor at a 60 percent discount.

Wholesale Prices, 1993

	Suggested Retail	Amount Realized after Wholesale Discount		Actual Wicker Costs
		50%	60%	
2-person basket	$ 95	$47.50	$ 38	$ 40
4-person basket	180	90.00	72	75
8-person basket	350	175.00	140	145

Evaluating the Opportunity

This is a typical marketing pricing problem; it involves the costs of production, break-even prices, established wholesale discount schedules, and suggested retail prices. On the surface, this distribution opportunity appears to expand the company's reach and to increase sales of its products. However, the offer as it stands would increase distribution and sales without increasing Wicker Industries' profits. The company would lose money because the 60 percent discount to the distributor results in a return that is less than its actual costs!

Looking for Options

To see if this deal can be made to work, start with the objectives for Wicker Industries. This is an emerging business that was created by its owner as a side business to his career as an engineer with an oil company. He hopes to build up Wicker Industries and to retire from the oil company in three years. Therefore, he feels that the company needs to find profitable strategies to expand the distribution of its baskets.

Next, look at how realistic the cost information is. An inexperienced business manager may be tempted to take the deal as it is because the company comes close to breaking even. The rationale might be that this is a marketing strategy to get "a foot in the door." However, this is where many businesses get into trouble. For each sale made through this distributor, Wicker loses money. It cannot ascribe this deliberate loss to marketing costs. The deal won't work—*as it stands.*

Four strategies to adjust the above price structure may make the offer more acceptable. These strategies can be applied individually or together to most of the close pricing decisions you will encounter.

- *Negotiate with the distributor* to arrive at a different discount schedule and to guarantee a minimum number of sales at or just above the company's break-even point. In addition, Wicker should identify a back-up market (sometimes called a remainder market), which would pay at least cost for any overruns or remainder items in discontinued lines of baskets. It is always a good idea to identify a "worst case" option.
- *Review the company price/profit strategies* to reflect a different break-even point. For example, if you're using cost/plus pricing, consider moving from a cost/plus 20 percent profit ratio strategy to a cost/plus 25 percent or 30 percent profit ratio.
- *Make adjustments in the product,* using same or similar components. In this product, Wicker could use less expensive but still good-quality dishes, flatware, linens, and containers.
- *Reduce costs further* by seeking quantity discounts from other suppliers. In this case, Wicker could buy the dishes, and other materials in bulk and negotiate with its suppliers for a better price. This leaves the risk that it may not be able to sell all of the increased inventory. Wicker could also check other suppliers for better prices.

If Wicker Industries is serious about offering its picnic baskets regionally, the opportunity could be a good one. However, it should pursue all of these suggestions to increase profit, reduce costs, and offer the product at a price that seems appropriate to the wholesaler/distributor market. If one of the objectives of this company is to increase the distribution area from tri-state to regional, the possibility of using a distributor who reaches a wider area should not be ignored. There may be other options that would allow Wicker Industries to make a profit and still expand the geographic placement of its products.

Procedures for Setting Prices

Most business managers know intuitively that success depends on a mix of profitable prices and the ability to adjust those prices to the needs of the target market, the objectives of the company, and competitive offerings. Research, judgment, and analysis of existing products' prices can help you narrow your pricing options.

STRATEGIC PLAYSHEET 11.

Example Determining Price for ______________ Company

Time Management Consultant

1. Estimate the demand by looking closely at your target markets. You can use past sales of similar products—yours, the industry's, or your competitors'. What do you estimate the demand for your products to be? *As area companies begin to hire more outside consultants, demand exceeds ability to service*

2. Look at your competition chart in Chapter 3. Is there a price leader, one company that appears to be #1? *Yes, Timely Issues* If so, are your prices in line with those of similar products? *No, I am lower.* Are territories a factor? *Maybe*
   What are the general discount policies within your industry? *not applicable*
   What are the possible and probable reactions of your competitors to your pricing? *I am not now a threat*

3. In view of the target market's needs and the strength and number of competitors in your field, what is your current market share? *5%* What do you expect this plan to do to that market share? *price combined with new distribution options will increase perceived value and market share (est. 8%)*

4. Look at your pricing strategy options in light of your company objectives for using the product life cycle. Are your products spread over all phases of the product life cycle, or are they bunched in one sector? What does this tell you? *My pricing strategy is to take advantage of the growth side of the industry product life cycle, e.g., higher prices while in growth mode with minimum competition.*

5. What is the price range that you determined in this chapter? *individual rate, $75 per hour; seminars, $40 per person*
   What is your break-even price? *$60 per hour; 25 participants @ $40 each.*
   Is there an opportunity to maintain perceived value of your products and cut costs? How? *not determined as yet unless preparation time is significantly reduced*

6. Select a pricing strategy: low prices/high volume or high prices/low volume. Compare your strategy with your objectives and the resources of your company; with the legal limitations or opportunities; with pricing ranges currently offered; and with the product-service offering of your company. State your strategy. *move from low price/high volume toward high price/low volume; raise prices to cover costs of new distribution system and to increase profit ratio*

7. Seek advice from your accountants and your sales people before setting a final price policy.
   Anticipated suggested retail price range: *individual, $100 per hour; seminars, $50 per person, minimum 35 participants; add base rate for speaker's bureau for keynote speaking*
   Anticipated wholesale discount percentage: *15% agent fee*

8. Monitor your sales, profits, and competitor reactions closely. Adjust if needed, but not frequently.

STRATEGIC PLAYSHEET 11.

Determining Price for ________________ Company

1. Estimate the demand by looking closely at your target markets. You can use past sales of similar products—yours, the industry's, or your competitors'. What do you estimate the demand for your products to be? ____________________

2. Look at your competition chart in Chapter 3. Is there a price leader, one company that appears to be #1? __________ If so, are your prices in line with those of similar products? __________ Are territories a factor? __________
   What are the general discount policies within your industry? __________

   What are the possible and probable reactions of your competitors to your pricing? __________

3. In view of the target market's needs and the strength and number of competitors in your field, what is your current market share? ______ What do you expect this plan to do to that market share? __________

4. Look at your pricing strategy options in light of your company objectives for using the product life cycle. Are your products spread over all phases of the product life cycle, or are they bunched in one sector? What does this tell you? __________

5. What is the price range that you determined in this chapter? __________

   What is your break-even price? __________
   Is there an opportunity to maintain perceived value of your products and cut costs? How? __________

6. Select a pricing strategy: low prices/high volume or high prices/low volume. Compare your strategy with your objectives and the resources of your company; with the legal limitations or opportunities; with pricing ranges currently offered; and with the product-service offering of your company. State your strategy. __________

7. Seek advice from your accountants and your sales people before setting a final price policy.
   Anticipated suggested retail price range: ____________________

   ____

   ____

   Anticipated wholesale discount percentage: ____________________

8. Monitor your sales, profits, and competitor reactions closely. Adjust if needed, but not frequently.

Strategy Check for Pricing Methods Selected

1. Name your target markets: ______________________________

____

____

____

2. Based on the products and services, what are your pricing strategy and price ranges? How will you implement these prices? ______________________________

____

____

____

3. Will this strategy work within the limitations you identified earlier?

EXTERNALLY LIMITING FACTORS:

Political and legal environment	Yes	No
Cultural and social environment	Yes	No
Economic environment	Yes	No
Technological environment	Yes	No
Competitive environment	Yes	No
Industrial environment	Yes	No

INTERNALLY DIRECTED FACTORS:

Goals and objectives	Yes	No
Ethics	Yes	No
Internal resources	Yes	No

4. State the objective this strategy will help to fulfill. ______________________________

____

____

____

8

Place Mix: Distribution Methods

Place Mix, the third P, considers the distribution and location factors you should consider when deciding how and where your customers will be able to purchase your products and services. Distribution is the method you use to get your products and services to your target market if its members cannot come to you, and location is the site your target market visits to purchase your products and services. To offer your products and services successfully to your target markets, you need at least an excellent location or an excellent distribution system. Ideally, you should consider having both options.

A distribution system includes all of the methods, businesses, and other links used to expedite the delivery of your products and services to the ultimate user. With the exception of a company sales force, your employees are not part of this system. The members of your network choose whether to carry your products or services to the markets that they influence; therefore, you should treat them as you would treat any important target market.

Businesses that perform distribution functions are referred to by a number of terms, including wholesalers, dealers, distributors, sales representatives, agents, brokers, auctioneers, jobbers, manufacturer's reps, merchants, retailers, shopkeepers, and vendors. Many of the terms are differentiated by details of contract arrangements or represent preferred industry terminology. For purposes of developing this marketing plan, we will use the following designations:

- *Retailers*—those persons whose primary business is to sell to and service the consumer market. Retailers usually collect sales tax on all purchases made by the individual consumer.
- *Wholesalers*—those persons whose primary business is to sell to other businesses, such as retailers, industry, or other commercial markets, but who do not sell to the final consumer market. Unless they sell to the public, as well as other businesses, wholesalers usually are not responsible for collecting sales tax.
- *Middlemen*—any business link between the manufacturer or service provider and the end consumer.

In this chapter, you will determine your distribution strategies. You will look at environmental factors that are external to your company and internal company factors that influence your decisions. You will determine the best routes for your company to reach its markets profitably.

General Distribution Strategies

Regardless of the type of business you are involved in, there are three broad general distribution strategies you should consider. They are:

- Intensive
- Selective
- Exclusive

Which strategy you use should be determined by your company's goals and objectives and by which allows you the best access to your target markets.

An *intensive distribution* strategy is often combined with a penetration pricing strategy to present your products and services through a wide variety of wholesalers and retailers to reach the broadest range of markets. A *selective distribution* strategy, in contrast, offers your products or services only through those wholesalers and retailers who do the best job of getting your products and services sold to your targeted markets. They either have the best access to your desired markets or are willing to place more emphasis on moving your products and services. Finally, an *exclusive distribution* strategy limits the placement of your products or services to one channel source in each geographic area. In exchange for the exclusive rights to sell your products or services in a region, the distributor usually guarantees the purchase of all or nearly all of your products or services allotted to that market area.

Externally Dictated Factors

Because each member of your distribution system represents a separate business, you need to consider marketing plans for attracting and choosing the best combination of alternatives. You must consider the effects of the externally dictated factors discussed in Chapter 3 and briefly review their possible implication for your distribution decisions.

- *Political and Legal Environment.* Place-distribution decisions, like pricing decisions, are highly regulated, particularly for interstate trade. Over the years, laws have been enacted to encourage competition, to guard against monopolies or conspiracies to control distribution channels, and to protect small businesses and consumers from potentially unethical practices. On the state and local levels, sales and property tax rates, zoning ordinances, and generally accepted contract practices of wholesalers will also influence your choices. If you have questions about a particular opportunity, check with your attorney.
- *Cultural and Social Environment.* Each industry has developed its own norms for conducting business. Business-to-business dealings may be as formal as written proposals or as informal as a handshake; sales to government agencies are usually

accomplished through "requests for proposals" and a bidding process. Knowing the customary business practices of your wholesalers helps you to position your products and services favorably.

The cultural and social environment for retailers has changed drastically in recent years. The "mom and pop" neighborhood store, the isolated department store, and door-to-door sales have been replaced by shopping malls offering entire cultural and social communities. Knowing the social context in which your final consumers shop will help you identify place limitations and opportunities for your marketing planning.

▪ *Economic Environment*. The economy of the country, region, and city influences both your consumer markets' ability to purchase your products or services and your wholesalers' needs and ability to carry your products or services. Make sure that your wholesalers and suppliers are financially able to deliver their services on a timely basis. Elasticity factors (discussed in Chapter 7), also influence this environment.

▪ *Technological Environment*. As technology develops, major changes occur in methods of production and distribution. The introduction of fax machines has altered order processes, sales calls and reporting, and research options, as well as numerous other functions that expedite the servicing of your final customers. Some middleman functions have been significantly reduced by this one innovation. Computer programs and cable shopping networks have also opened new routes for direct retailing. Advances in tracking final consumers' buying habits will make direct marketing a more desirable distribution choice aided by relatively inexpensive video equipment that assists in packaging services for sale and distribution to broader markets. Major marketing advances are being made by companies willing to research and adjust their place mix to meet the technology that is available.

▪ *Competitive Environment*. As you analyzed your competition in Chapter 3, you identified windows of opportunity. Competition is a major factor in your place-distribution decisions. Observe your competition and determine how you can use its choices of locations and/or distribution channels to your advantage. Continually monitor your competition for changes it is making in its efforts to bring its products and services to *your* markets.

▪ *Industrial Environment*. As noted in Chapter 3, this environment has developed two conflicting trends in recent years: (1) the move toward cooperation within industries, and (2) the trend toward fierce intra-industry competition. It is most important that you identify which trend your industry tends to follow, because this environment sets the stage for most of your marketing planning decisions. Much of your market's expectations about conducting business with you are based on the reputation of your industry, its policies and its general ethics.

Internally Directed Factors

Internally directed factors, discussed in Chapter 3, are those that form the company environment within which your marketing planning develops, receives budgeting, and is implemented. These factors are important in your place-distribution decisions in the following ways:

- *Company Goals and Objectives* determine the focus of your marketing plan and its distribution strategies. Marketing managers are frequently asked to develop plans to distribute products and services to substantially new and different markets. Because goals vary from company to company, your marketing plans must be developed specifically to meet your company's needs and stated goals.

- *Corporate Ethics* define codes of conduct for dealing within the company as well as working with your suppliers, wholesalers, retailers, and clients. Congruence between your personal and corporate standards for ethics and those of your markets and your industry minimize conflicts among distribution channels and enhance your working relationships.

- *Internal Resources* include capacity, equipment, inventory, manpower, and money. Your place-distribution choices of wholesalers and retailers can significantly enhance your available resources. Factors affecting distribution choice are discussed later in this chapter.

The Adjustables: Market Selections and Place-Distribution

Most emerging businesses deal directly with either other businesses or the individual consumer. As a business grows, it is unlikely that the owners or managers personally will be able to handle new target markets or territories and larger volume sales in the same manner as in the past. New methods of distributing products and services to target markets need to be explored.

When business managers think about marketing planning, they generally look first at advertising alternatives, then at pricing reductions, and finally at product modifications. Most managers assume that the distribution system is fixed. In fact, your business can often find significant and profitable windows of opportunity in new or novel approaches to distributing your products. For example, doing business by mail is taken for granted as a distribution technique. However, rapid changes in the pace of business and personal lives have encouraged new ways of getting products and services to the market quickly, and technological changes mean that the overnight delivery service, cable shopping services, computer modems, and fax machines must be considered as "new or improved" means of delivering information and offering products and services for sale.

In the 1990s, the impact of information and technological discoveries is likely to increase in our homes. Consumers in the 1990s expect quick delivery of products and services—and don't regard it as an extra.

Selecting the Appropriate Distribution Channel

As you look at the possible channels for distributing your products or services, think in terms of everyone involved, from the producer to the last person to purchase the product before significant changes to the product occur. For example, a bolt of cloth may go from the mill to the warehouse and distribution center to a retail fabric shop. It is still the same product. When that bolt leaves the fabric shop and becomes a dress, it is then a different product. Each middleman along the way can be a specific target market for your products or services. And each middleman has differing wants and needs for your products or services. Do not overlook the many possibilities for enhancing your products or services in the marketplace through the skillful use of middlemen.

Selecting the Appropriate Location

For many retail businesses, choice of location is the most significant factor of the marketing mix. Unfortunately, owners of new retail businesses often simply select the least expensive option. This can be a mistake for two reasons:

- It probably does not offer easy accessibility for your target market;
- An out-of-the-way location will require you to spend more on advertising, personal calling, and delivery costs to increase foot traffic and to service your target market.

The perceived value of your location choice enhances or diminishes the worth of your products and services in the eyes of your target market. You should seek a location in an area where a large number of your potential customers already go for similar kinds of business activities.

You want to locate where your target markets locate. In retailing, for instance, it is essential to be near competitor businesses; shoe stores locate near other shoe stores to increase the traffic of shoppers "in the market" for shoes. For medical practices, desirable locations are those near other physicians who offer complementary skills and within a few minutes from your main hospital. For a professional service business, an office in the business district near banks and other professionals can be a positive location choice; a manufacturer may want to consider an industrial area or a developed industrial park where access to rail, truck lines, and other methods for shipping and receiving will be easy.

Factors Affecting Distribution Choice

Accessibility

Your primary concern in making place-distribution choices is that the location or distribution method provide easy access to your target market. You may have the best product and service at the best price available, and it may fit your market's needs perfectly. However, without an accessible location or distribution system for your products and services, you will never be able to sell them.

Desired Functions

In addition to providing a method for your customers to purchase your products and services, your location or place and your distribution system may offer a wide variety of functions. Typically, these involve:

- Transportation and delivery
- Promotion
- Storage
- Credit to buyers
- Ability to combine goods from several sources
- Presence or image
- Safety and protection
- Packaging
- Assembly
- Collection
- Time and cost efficiencies
- Market research information
- Friendly business advice

Choosing a middleman or a new method of distribution is like including a new partner in your enterprise. The method needs to be an extension of your business and its philosophy.

Creative Options for Services

In most industries, new approaches to placing, moving, scheduling, locating, and assigning—whatever your industry calls distribution—can help your business prosper. This is true for service industries as well as for products.

Additional markets for services have been found by increasing service availability during specified times or nonpeak hours. Trade associations have assisted their member businesses by distributing services through creative outlets; for example, hotels offer complimentary pick-up and delivery of guests' shoes for shoe shines after 10 P.M., allowing better use of hotel night staff and/or an opportunity for local shoe shine vendors to subcontract work through the hotels. Similarly, accounting professionals provide incentives to clients who schedule audits at nonpeak times during the business year. Such scheduling equalizes the work schedule for the accountants and also assures personal attention for the clients. Attorneys create similar plans to encourage clients to prepare wills and estate plans at generally slow times of the year, and may offer educational seminars on business and consumer issues through their bar association.

Examples of creative service distribution abound. Ski-slope operators have moved their ski storage service from closets in hotels and rental shops to the base of many of their slopes, encouraging the skier to return to their slopes the next day rather than ski others in the vicinity. Car washers, mechanics, and dry cleaners are among the service businesses that offer pick-up and delivery for occupants of office buildings during office hours. The availability of services makes the office buildings more desirable locations for businesses, is a great convenience for those who work in the buildings, and helps the service businesses target people who may not otherwise use them.

Services delivered or performed for the elderly in their homes include everything from check-writing, beauty-shop services, and physical therapy to grocery delivery. These may all be scheduled by the provider at times that do not conflict with the schedules of other groups of customers. More visible creative options for distributing products and services include the store and nonstore methods listed in Planning Exercise 8-1. (Many nonstore distribution methods are also forms of promotion, to be discussed in the following chapter.)

Planning Exercise 8-1.
Identifying Channels of Distribution

In the list below, check all the ways in which your customers currently receive your products or services. Also check any additional methods you would like to use to serve your target market.

Sample List of Distribution Methods

Method	*Current Use*	*Future Use*
Nonstore Methods		
Auctions		
Bazaars		
Brokers and agents		
Catalogs		
Catalog showrooms		
Caterers		
Computer shopping		
Delivery services		
Direct response merchandising		
"800" telephone numbers		
flyers		
reply cards		
TV and cable shopping		
Farmers' markets		
In-home retailing		
demonstrations		
mail		
telephone/telemarketing		
Membership requirements		
Mobile demonstration facilities		
Mobile offices		
Professionals		
Schools		
Trade shows		
Vending machines, carts, vans		
Store Methods		
Boutiques		
Buying services		
Convenience stores		
Department stores		
Discount stores		
Factory outlets		
Membership warehouses		
Specialty stores		
Stores–Retail		
Stores–Wholesale		
Supermarkets		
discount supermarkets		
hypermarkets		
Variety stores		
Warehouse showrooms		

STRATEGIC PLAYSHEET 12.

Example Selecting Distribution Methods

Business Center Catering Service

Review this list of questions before settling on the appropriate place to sell your products and services.

1. Market Considerations
   As you did with the other two Ps, product and price, start with your target markets.
   Where are they located? *corporations & businesses in downtown area*
   How can you most easily get your products and/or services to them?
   personal delivery and set-up
   Are several territories involved or only one? *1*
   What is the potential number of customers? *500–1000*
   What is their usual order size? *8 to 12 lunches*
   Who buys your products and services? *requested by professionals, ordered by secretaries*
   How often do they buy them? *varies*
   Why do they buy them? *convenience for working lunch meetings*

2. Product-Service Considerations
   What marketing logistics are required to handle the product or service? *on-site kitchen facilities—minimum cold capabilities*
   Is it perishable? Or does it have a long shelf-life? *perishable*
   Is it technical in nature, requiring specialized installation or explanation? *no, but requires service*
   What is its size? Is it large and bulky or neatly packaged, a dozen to a box? *box lunch specials packaged individually or full 6 course meals*
   Is mail a consideration? *N/A* How much does it weigh? *N/A*

3. Company Considerations
   What are your goals and objectives for this product or service? *to profitably cater the meeting needs of the business community*
   What services are you willing to offer? *menu selection, preparation, delivery, set-up, service, & clean-up*
   Are you limited to one location? *no—just area*
   How much control over distribution do you seek? Do you want the product to be uniquely available through your sales force, or do you want it widely available through various outlets or methods? *available only through catering office*
   Where are you located in relation to your target market?
   same area
   Does another middleman have better access to that market? *no*
   Are there legal or cultural issues to consider? *legal—health inspections and licenses*

4. Make your distribution choices here. Try to think of at least two different ways in which you could profitably get your products or services to your selected target market.

1. *Deliver to office—full service*
2. *Pick-up point for take-out via fax*
3. ______
4. ______

STRATEGIC PLAYSHEET 12.

Selecting Distribution Methods for ______________ Company

Review this list of questions before settling on the appropriate place to sell your products and services.

1. Market Considerations
   As you did with the other two Ps, product and price, start with your target markets.
   Where are they located? ______________
   How can you most easily get your products and/or services to them?
   ____
   Are several territories involved or only one? ______________
   What is the potential number of customers? ______________
   What is their usual order size? ______________
   Who buys your products and services? ______________
   ____
   How often do they buy them? ______________
   Why do they buy them? ______________

2. Product-Service Considerations
   What marketing logistics are required to handle the product or service?
   ____
   Is it perishable? Or does it have a long shelf-life? ______________
   Is it technical in nature, requiring specialized installation or explanation?
   ____
   What is its size? Is it large and bulky or neatly packaged, a dozen to a box?
   ____
   Is mail a consideration? ________ How much does it weigh? ______________

3. Company Considerations
   What are your goals and objectives for this product or service?
   ____
   What services are you willing to offer?
   ____
   Are you limited to one location? ______________
   How much control over distribution do you seek? Do you want the product to be uniquely available through your sales force, or do you want it widely available through various outlets or methods? ______________
   ____
   Where are you located in relation to your target market? ______________
   ____
   Does another middleman have better access to that market? ______________
   Are there legal or cultural issues to consider? ______________

4. Make your distribution choices here. Try to think of at least two different ways in which you could profitably get your products or services to your selected target market.

1. ______________________ 3. ______________________

2. ______________________ 4. ______________________

____

Strategy Check for Distribution Methods

1. Name your target markets: ______________________________

____

____

____

____

2. Based on the products and services and price ranges for these markets, what is your distribution strategy? How will you make your products and services available to these markets? ______________________________

____

____

____

____

3. Will this strategy work within the limitations you identified earlier?

EXTERNALLY LIMITING FACTORS:

Political and legal environment	Yes	No
Cultural and social environment	Yes	No
Economic environment	Yes	No
Technological environment	Yes	No
Competitive environment	Yes	No
Industrial environment	Yes	No

INTERNALLY DIRECTED FACTORS:

Goals and objectives	Yes	No
Ethics	Yes	No
Internal resources	Yes	No

4. State the objective this strategy will help to fulfill. ______________________________

____

____

____

9

Promotion Mix

Promotion, the final P in your marketing mix, is often mistaken for the entire marketing process. In reality, promotion decisions are the last part of the process, but often the most visible part. The effectiveness of the promotion for any product or service hinges on how well you chose your target markets and on how well you planned your products, prices, and distribution methods to meet the common needs of several of those target markets.

Promotion, in its simplest form, is how you tell your target markets what you want them to know, encourage them to do what you want them to do, and remind them to do it. You communicate with your target markets about your products and services through the elements of promotion that you choose. Your marketing plan began with specific objectives (see Chapter 4). As you develop your promotional ideas, remember these rules of thumb:

- The purposes of promotion are to educate, encourage or persuade, and remind.
- Promotion works best when you identify the common needs of your target markets and base your message on the benefits of your products and services that satisfy those needs.
- The elements of promotion are the vehicle through which your message is carried to your markets.
- The buying process involves distinct stages that begin before a purchase is made.
- Promotion provides quick and repetitive information to your target markets. Repeat the same message to your target markets at least three to four times.
- You must evaluate your promotional efforts to determine how well you have met your stated objectives.

Everyone has an idea of what promotion is, what it should or should not do, what is good or bad about it. We tend to see and judge this very public part of business in terms of our own experience, rather than through specific knowledge of basic concepts and terminology. Because target markets expect communication from businesses through promotion, very few businesses can become profitable without using some forms of promotion. Your target markets need to know about your company and its products and services before they can beat a path to your door.

Elements of Promotion

Many components go into a promotional plan. Your particular plan may use one element or combine several ways of reaching your target market.

Personal Selling

This includes any sales message that is relayed through the sales force, the management, or the owners of your company. It also includes any sales messages relayed by representatives and agents for your company. To be successful, any form of personal selling must be carefully planned. Personal selling is the most expensive promotional tool, but it is also the most effective; it is worth the cost when your company is offering expensive items or services or when your products and services need a great deal of explanation.

Methods of personal selling include:

- Face-to-face sales calls
- Telephone contacts
- Special events
- Cause-related coalitions
- Store contacts
- Telemarketing
- Trade shows
- Bazaars
- Mobile offices
- Showrooms

Direct Mail

This method includes any promotional message relayed to your target markets through any form of mail. Direct mail varies in cost but tends to be expensive because it requires developing a mail piece, preparing it for mailing, and paying the mailing costs. The success of direct mail depends on the appropriateness of your mailing list and the quality of the communication mailed and how well it promotes your product's benefits to your market.

Direct mail pieces often include action-response forms that need to be explained. The usual rate of return for a mailing to a well-targeted list is between ½ percent and 2 percent of the total number of pieces mailed. Repeating the same mailing to the same list within a short period of time can increase its effectiveness greatly. Because direct mail is used so frequently, you generally have less than ten seconds to gain customers' attention before they trash your promotion. Remember that for some, perhaps all, of your customers, the direct-mail promotion is the only representation of your product and service that they see.

Methods of direct mail include:

- Brochures
- Letters
- Newsletters
- Catalogs
- Postcards
- Flyers
- Samples
- Fax transmissions

Incentives

This promotional tool includes small "freebies" and opportunities to make special purchases with a minimum purchase (purchase with a purchase). The cost of incentives varies widely; they are most often used with other elements of promotion, increasing the expense. Incentives are used to thank customers for their business, to encourage customers to try a product or service, to add a benefit to your product or service, and to increase company name recognition among target market groups. Incentives are often creative and fun methods to promote your business. The success of incentives really depends on your objectives for using them. It's very easy to overdo this promotional method. Use caution and reason to match the possible incentive with the target market's self-image and desires in order to maintain the tactic's effectiveness.

Methods of using incentives include:

- Gifts
- Purchase with a purchase
- Samples
- Coupons
- Rebates
- Awards
- Recognitions
- Rewards

Visuals: Signs, business cards, stationery products

People don't often think of signs, business cards, and stationery products as important communication and sales tools. In our sophisticated world, we receive so much visual input that we tend to overlook many things. It is simply imperative to use the best visuals that you can to compete with all the other information in the marketplace. Your company needs signs, business cards, and stationery products, anyway, so make the best use of your business expenses by developing a consistent graphic design. Visuals can provide a consistent image and can graphically unite your various messages.

Methods of using visuals include:

- Signs
- Business cards
- Stationery
- Billing statements
- All promotional materials
- Training materials
- Contracts
- Equipment
- Name tags
- Packaging
- Report covers

Publicity

This element includes any public media coverage your company obtains free of charge. There is no direct cost for publicity from the media. However, you may incur the costs of developing an event, sending press releases, writing articles, and giving speeches or hiring a publicist to carry out these functions. Publicity coverage is considered valuable because it carries with it an implied endorsement from the media. However, companies cannot rely solely on successful use of publicity because they have no control over what is said nor when coverage is disseminated.

Methods of using publicity include:

- Print media
- Newspapers
- Magazines
- Trade journals
- Newsletters
- Grocery sacks
- Electronic media
- Television
- Radio
- Computer
- Movies
- Newsreels/programs
- Word-of-mouth
- Staged events

Many other methods of publicity are open to your company.

Advertising

This tool is the element that comes to mind first when a company is considering its marketing plan and promotions. Advertising includes all impersonal, paid, openly sponsored forms of communication about your company and its products and services. It includes messages in print or electronic media, or placed on bus benches, bus or taxi cards, posters, banners, airplane or blimp banners, billboards, signs in lobbies, directories, airport booths, and maps (see Figure 9-1). In general, the public does not consider these vehicles as trustworthy as the implied endorsement that you get from publicity. However, with advertising, you can control the message and the media choice completely. You must pay for advertising, of course, and it can be very expensive. When you decide to use advertising for your company, be very clear about your expectations. The more specific your objectives are, the better you will be able to design your message and measure your results.

Outlets for advertising include:

- Newspapers
- Radio
- Television
- Direct mail
- Cable TV
- Signs
- Trade journals
- Magazines
- Outdoor/transit
- Computer access
- Information service
- Coupon books
- Posters
- Banners
- Maps
- Events
- Books
- Airport booths
- Billboards
- Directories
- Movies
- Seminars

Buyer Behavior

Studies of consumer psychology reveal that buyers go through distinct stages before they actually purchase a product or service. These stages are:

Figure 9-1. Comparison* of major advertising options by selected characteristics.

Selected Traits	*Newspaper*	*Radio*	*TV*	*Magazines*	*Outdoor Transit*	*Direct Mail*	*Computer*
REACH	broad	medium	broad	specific	broad	specific	growing
FREQUENCY	good	excellent	excellent	poor	good	moderate	on demand
COLOR	average-good	none	excellent	excellent	good	good-excellent	poor
GROSS INVESTMENT	moderate	low	high	moderate	low	high	high
ENVIRONMENT FOR MESSAGE	home/office	home/auto	home	home/office	auto/transit	home/office	home/office

*These vary greatly nationally, depending on the specific medium and market.

1. *Awareness*. Consumers become aware of the product's or service's existence and of companies that may offer it.
2. *Interest*. Buyers develop some feeling that the product may be useful or beneficial to them. They may be sensitive to factual information about the product or service.
3. *Desire*. They may actually want the product or service and look favorably at the benefits that they may gain.
4. *Action*. They purchase and use the product or service.
5. *Post-Purchase Behavior*. Buyers seek confirmation that they have made the right choice. They look for reinforcement of the benefits.

NOTE: These are not progressive stages. Buyers usually flip-flop back and forth between each stage.

Communication Through Promotions

If you have adequately defined your target market and its needs, your promotion options will be defined by using the promotion formula (see page 111). Remember that all your promotion efforts should be part of an ongoing communication process with your markets (see Figure 9-2).

Promotion starts with translating your company's objectives into a message that explains how products and services can meet your target market's needs and wants. The key to developing an effective promotional message is to identify the needs of your target markets and to design your message around the benefits that satisfy the common needs of the most important markets. The creative part of this process is knowing how to match the necessary message with the appropriate promotional elements for your target market to hear, understand, and act on.

Figure 9-3 gives examples of appropriate messages for each buyer behavior stage as well as suggestions of choices of promotion elements to carry those messages to your target markets.

Figure 9-2. The communication process.

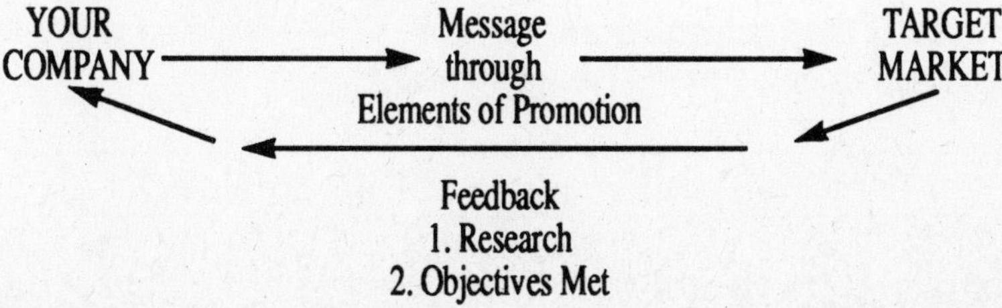

Figure 9-3. Buyer behavior states with message and promotion suggestions.

Sales Process State	*Message Likely Used*	*Promotion Choices*
AWARENESS	Messages describe general information about company: Name Address Telephone/Fax General product information	Publicity Telephone Directory listings Signs Some ads (if budget allows)
INTEREST	Messages describe product-service features and benefits, reasons to investigate or try products-services	Above, plus: Specific ads Sales promotions Trade discounts Personal selling
DESIRE	Messages aimed at confirmation that your products are preferred choice; testimonials	Same options, plus word-of-mouth Telemarketing (if budget allows)
ACTION	Messages give reason to act now; seek closure; offer rebates, incentive; displays, catalogs, coupons, dealer discounts	Personal selling Telemarketing Direct mail Point of Purchase
POST-PURCHASE	Messages reinforce buyer's decision; continued follow-up service	Personal selling Direct mail Telemarketing Advertising Public relations

Planning Exercise 9-1.
Steps to Develop Your Promotions

1. Select Target Markets
   The target markets must be selected carefully. They must have the ability to do what you want and to render the results that are desired. They must also be willing to do those things. Place the name of the target markets here:
   1. ____________________
   2. ____________________
   3. ____________________

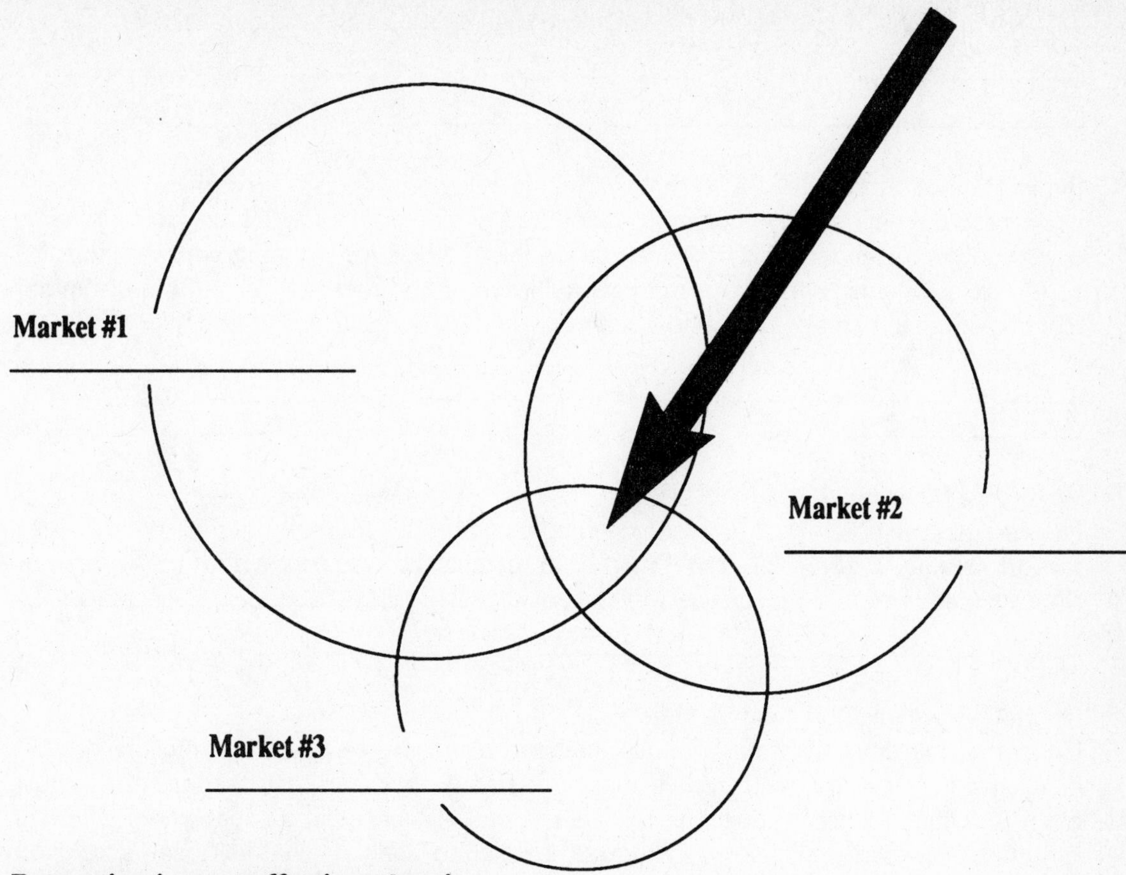

Promotion is most effective when it is aimed at the overlapping needs of your target markets.

2. Identify Needs and Benefits
   What are the overlapping needs and desires of the above target markets? To make the greatest impact on your target markets, talk to them about the benefits that they will receive based on their needs. This approach helps you access their desire for the benefits of your product-service.
   What are the common needs of your target markets?
   1. ______________________________
   2. ______________________________
   3. ______________________________

   What benefits satisfy those needs?
   1. ______________________________
   2. ______________________________
   3. ______________________________

3. State Specific Objectives
   The desired outcome is a specific objective with measurable results. Be sure to assess whether it is realistic to expect this target market to grant your wishes. What specific objectives are you seeking?

4. Select Promotion Vehicles
   Now that you know what you want from your target markets, check the available elements of promotion to see which is the most reasonable method for reaching your markets. Be sure to select a vehicle that your markets will listen to and that they trust for information. Choose your elements of promotion here:

5. Write Your Message
   How do you ask your target market for what you want? Tell them about their benefits with a short message causing the target market to react in the way you wish it to. Write your message here:

6. Continue Research and Analyze Feedback
   Consumer reactions must be carefully analyzed to see if you are achieving the desired effect. How do you know if you've met your stated objectives? By feedback, the most often forgotten part of the formula. This is unfortunate, because feedback holds the key to future successful promotions. Without the ability to analyze what has been successful or unsuccessful in the past, you eliminate the possibility of learning from both your mistakes and your successes.
   A professional marketing person understands and uses feedback and is not threatened by it. List any feedback you have from the current promotion here:

Promotion Formula

Because developing promotional strategies is and should be such a creative and fun process, many of us forget some or several of the critical steps. In order to see if the promotion you designed is likely to meet your objectives, use this promotion formula; it will help focus your energies and remind you of the steps involved in successful promotional strategy-building.

Planning Exercise 9-2
Promotion Formula

This formula is designed to ensure that your promotional strategies have taken into account all steps to successful sales.

MESSAGE COMMUNICATED THROUGH MEDIA/MEDIUM

1. ______________________
2. ______________________
3. ______________________

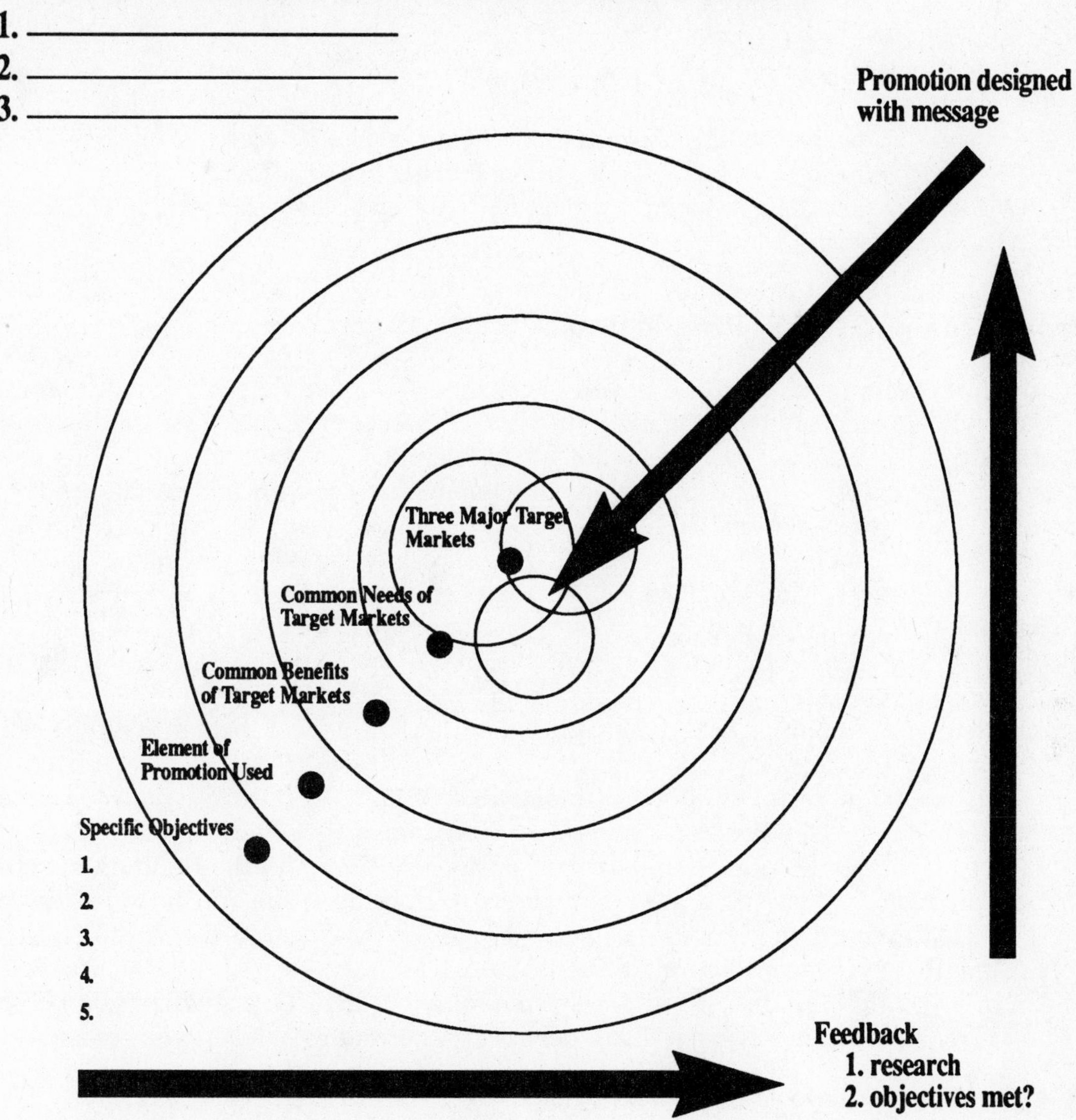

STRATEGY SUMMARY: ____

____

____

____

On the promotion formula diagram, follow the process described to track your message and the chosen medium. (Start at the top right and move counterclockwise.)

Process for Checking Your Promotions

- What is your message?
- Is the message appropriate for your target markets?
- Does the message address the needs of your target markets?
- Does the message specify the benefits to your target markets?
- Is the element of promotion used both appropriate and trustworthy for your target markets?
- Is the promotion strategy designed to meet your specific objectives.
- Does the feedback indicate that the promotion has been successful?
- How are you going to incorporate this feedback and other research into your next marketing plan?

Promotion and the Selling Process

At any given time, there are only so many businesses or consumers within your target markets who are actually in the market for your products or services. In order for your products and services to be considered when members of your target market are actually in the market, your company needs to maintain a presence, a certain level of visibility. This presence is created by the use of "the drip system," regularly scheduled promotions that familiarize your target markets with your company name and its products or services. This familiarity creates the awareness and level of comfort your markets need to consider your products or services when they are ready to buy. To encourage purchases, you should increase the frequency of promotions just prior to peak buying cycles and, at other times, adjust your product-service, price, place-distribution, and promotion schedule to address other markets or meet different needs of your original markets.

On the diagram in Figure 9-4, X indicates a promotion during a specified time period. A cluster of Xs indicates a heavy promotion and sales period.

Larger companies often combine their business vision with the common benefit of their products or services to several markets to develop a slogan. By consistently using a slogan with their company name and logo (or typeface) in their promotions, they establish a presence. (Figure 9.5 lists some well-known examples.) If you have a slogan or if you develop one, it's important to remember that it's just when you begin to get sick of hearing and seeing it that it begins to work and establishes your presence.

Does your company have a slogan? If so, write it here. ______________________________

____

If not, can you develop a slogan by combining your company's vision with one or more common benefits which your products or services offer to your target markets? __________

____

____

Consult Table 9-1 for ideas.

Figure 9-4. "The drip system."

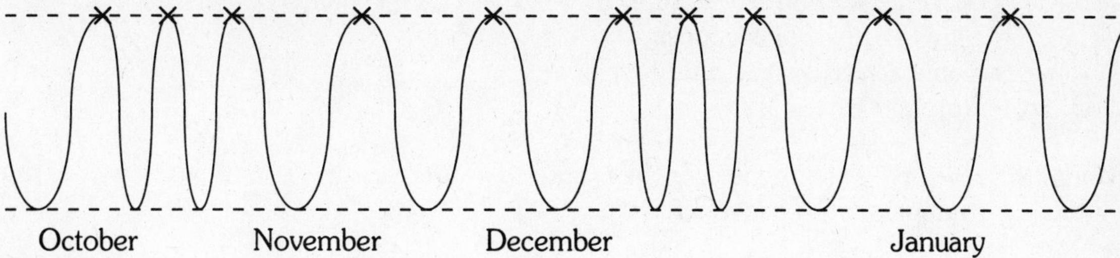

Figure 9-5. The creative solution.

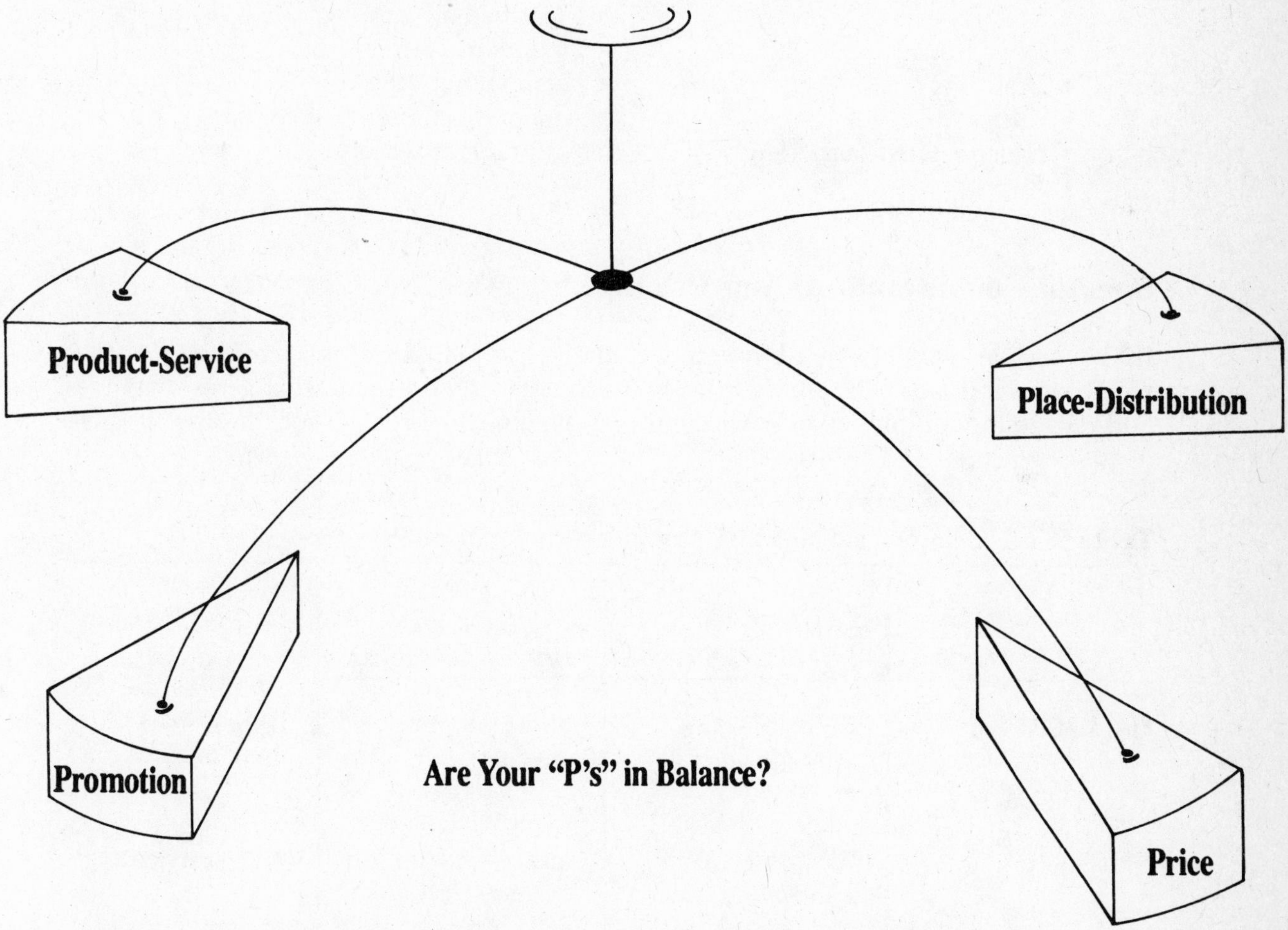

Product-Service

Place-Distribution

Promotion

Are Your "P's" in Balance?

Price

Special Consideration: Promotions Within a Small Budget

Needing to promote a product or service within the confines of a small budget is a common problem. There are many things that you can do to promote your business without spending all your profits on promotion.

Businesses whose promotion objectives are to develop awareness and to maintain a presence often use the following minimum methods of promotion:

- Publicity
- Ads in telephone directories
- Signs at place of business
- Some advertising, if budget allows
- Employee networks

When the objective is to encourage the markets to purchase the product or service, the following strategies often prove effective:

- Publicity
- Business cards
- Simple brochures or flyers
- Coupons
- Open houses
- Drawings
- Sales
- Cause-related marketing
- Awards
- Newsletters
- Cooperative advertising
- Trade association sources
- Classified advertising
- Statement stuffers
- Personal networks
- Any existing points of contact with target markets

Special Consideration: New Product Introduction Example

In this section, we present a hypothetical marketing plan for a new product, Compu-bag, a new golf bag with a built-in mini computer, Compu-score, that gives distances and related topography from any location on the course to the hole. Compu-score also

Table 9-1. Common slogans that promote common benefits.

COMPANY	*SLOGAN*	*COMMON BENEFIT BASED ON NEED*	*POSSIBLE VISION*
HALLMARK	Care enough to send the very best . . .	buyer and receiver are special	highest % of market
DELTA	We love to fly and it shows . . .	quality and fun	#1 in service
COKE	The real thing . . .	original and best	# 1 in industry
FORD	Has a better idea . . .	innovation	best American carmaker
FROSTED FLAKES	They're greeeeeat!!!	good taste	great cereal maker

suggests possible clubs and strategies that might be useful for the golfer. Its automatic calculator simplifies scorekeeping, tracks handicaps, and compares individual scores for up to one hundred successive games. Compu-score keeps scores for up to four people. It is designed to be sold separately as well as with the new Compu-bag.

Company: The company is an established golf bag manufacturer with a product line that includes seventeen models of golf bags for both men and women.

Markets: The company sells its products to retailers through its own sales force (company sales representatives). Its wholesale accounts include sporting goods stores, golf course pro shops, resort area shops, and catalogs. The company also sells its products directly to the golfer/consumer through direct mail, advertising, and walk-in sales at the factory.

Because Compu-score represents a major diversification from golf bags, the company needs to develop a new marketing strategy for this product. This should be done two to three years in advance of debut. Compu-score's additional markets might include distributors, in addition to company sales reps, and gift markets.

Eighteen Months Before a Major Product Debuts

1. Review results of product research, including test market results. Update marketing plan and time-line schedule.
2. Develop an internal public relations plan to inform and involve your employees. Create opportunities for feedback. Use their expertise and input in order to fine-tune the product and possible promotions.
3. Have financial and marketing managers analyze costs, suggest retail prices and wholesale discounts, and develop a sales forecast.

Twelve Months Before Debut Date

1. Finalize marketing plans and budgets for each target market: present accounts, new distributors, and new retail outlets.
2. Implement the marketing plan as scheduled.
3. Begin implementing strategy for introduction to existing accounts. Encourage advance orders.

Six to Twelve Months Before Debut Date

1. Finalize your advertising and PR plans. Because this is a technologically advanced product and because it represents a major diversification for this well-known company, the possibilities for publicity are exceptional.
2. Begin implementation.
3. Make a detailed time line to schedule events, appearances, spot announcements for TV and radio, and any demonstrations. Disseminate this information to your employees.
4. Train your employees about the features and benefits of your new products. They need to know the current trends and why your products were developed to take advantage of those trends. This is an opportunity to take advantage of management techniques, including employee participation.
5. Organize your product demonstrations and prepare a videotape of your product for your sales reps and distributors.
6. Finalize your wholesale and retail mailing lists and other printed materials.

Four to Five Months Before Debut Date

1. Start taking orders from current and new accounts.
2. If you can get coverage in the media about Compu-bag and Compu-score and their development, do so. Be careful not to use up your alloted coverage for the year from any one PR source; you will want as much coverage as possible when your product or service is available to sell.
3. Review your time line of events. Finalize any plans for pro-amateur golf sponsorships or demonstrations near your introductory date.

Three Months Before Debut Date

1. Complete all your promotional printing: brochures, media kits, other printed pieces.
2. Mail brochures, order forms, etc., to your wholesale accounts. Also mail retail brochures and company catalogs.
3. Gather endorsements from local/regional/national celebrities and use them with your printed and visual materials.
4. Keep everyone informed on how you're doing. Keep up the momentum.
5. Make assignments. Schedule small events during debut week and during initial delivery. Set delivery schedule to stores. (This is likely to be a very hot item. Therefore, you will want to prioritize your deliveries and demonstrations.)
6. Check your budget and manpower needs. If you bring on additional people, don't forget to keep them up to date on your products.

Two Months Before Debut Date

1. Check with advertising and PR people to make sure that everything is being implemented as planned and is on schedule.
2. Finalize kick-off event(s). Work with other sponsors of pro-am tournament.
3. Take a crash course in stress management. At this point Murphy's Law tends to take over.
4. Continue support of company sales reps and distributors as they solicit accounts through printed materials and video.
5. Be sure to thank your people and share credit for successes.

One Month Before Debut Date

1. Finalize radio and TV appearances. (The schedules will all change at least once before the actual date.)
2. Check production and delivery schedules.
3. Review contingency plans.

One to Two Weeks Before Debut Date

1. Check to make sure that all products and related materials are in and accounted for.
2. Have a small celebration for your employees. If they prepurchased the Compu-bag and/or Compu-score, let them have the products in advance of the general public.

3. Pre-address and label all current product orders for shipping day. You may have to schedule special pickups with UPS or your freight company for initial shipments.

Debut Week

1. Your PR people should be available to meet, greet, and talk on the telephone at the office. Good people skills are a must.
2. Try to stay calm. Things will undoubtedly go wrong.
3. Have a good time and enjoy yourself. This is what you have been working so hard for.
4. Remember your workers, their families, and any volunteers. Give them credit for pulling off this successful promotion.

You have just launched not only two great products but an ongoing promotional cycle for the life of these products. Every time you celebrate a major anniversary or milestone, you have an opportunity to increase promotions, which should increase sales.

One to Six Months After Debut

1. Record all feedback from company sales reps, current accounts, and individuals.
2. Review current marketing plan, with special attention to competitor reaction and market share analysis.
3. Update your marketing plan, based on your research.

Summary of Promotion Selection

The seven-step promotion process that is the basis for a successful promotion campaign is predicated on targeting the correct market—one that is both able and willing to return to you whatever it is that you wish to have from it, in an amount that is in line with your specified objectives. The promotion process also depends on your ability to design and implement a strategy that will cause the market to act in a certain way. Putting this final P together with the products, prices, and place-distribution choices requires a creative balance in your planning process (see Figure 9-5). You must take into account not only your internal resources but the skill with which you can develop a succinct, persuasive message. Judge your effectiveness by your results and build on those answers.

STRATEGIC PLAYSHEET 13.

Example Promotion Selection Process for *Compu-Bag and Compu-Score* **Company**

Consider the following questions BEFORE you develop your message:

1. Place the name of the target markets here:
   pro shops *sporting goods catalogs*
   sporting goods stores
2. What are the common needs of your target markets?
   high quality, leading-edge products for their golfing customers, profitable margins, "giftable" items
3. What benefits satisfy those needs?
   our reputation for manufacturing quality products, newest technological product available, unique, exclusive appeal, newest quality gift item available for the golfer
4. What specific objectives are you seeking? What do you want the target markets to do?
   15 advance orders per current account three months prior to introduction of Compu-bag and Compu-score
5. What are the most direct routes for communicating with your target markets? Choose your elements of promotion here:
   personal sales through company sales reps using our new demonstration video; also direct mail, e.g., letter and brochure of introduction
6. In fifteen words or less, write your message here:
   Introducing Compu-bag and Compu-score—the newest, most unique and technologically advanced gift for any golfer
7. List any feedback you have from the current promotion here:
   new product—none yet

At this point you may decide to start all over or you may decide to go on to other markets or another promotion strategy for these markets.

STRATEGIC PLAYSHEET 13.

Promotion Selection Process for ____________________________ Company

Consider the following questions BEFORE you develop your message:

1. Place the name of the target markets here:

____

____

2. What are the common needs of your target markets?

____

____

3. What benefits satisfy those needs?

____

____

4. What specific objectives are you seeking? What do you want the target markets to do?

____

____

5. What are the most direct routes for communicating with your target markets? Choose your elements of promotion here:

____

____

____

6. In fifteen words or less, write your message here:

____

____

7. List any feedback you have from the current promotion here:

____

____

____

____

At this point you may decide to start all over or you may decide to go on to other markets or another promotion strategy for these markets.

____

Strategy Check for Promotion Methods Selected

1. Name your target markets: ______________________________

____

____

____

2. Based on the products and services, price ranges and distribution methods which you have selected for these markets, what is your promotion strategy? How will you communicate your message to the markets? ______________________________

____

____

____

3. Will this strategy work within the limitations you identified earlier?

EXTERNALLY LIMITING FACTORS:

Political and legal environment	Yes	No
Cultural and social environment	Yes	No
Economic environment	Yes	No
Technological environment	Yes	No
Competitive environment	Yes	No
Industrial environment	Yes	No

INTERNALLY DIRECTED FACTORS:

Goals and objectives	Yes	No
Ethics	Yes	No
Internal resources	Yes	No

4. State the objective this strategy will help to fulfill. ______________________________

____

____

____

The Financial Solutions: Your Marketing Budgets

10

Marketing Budgets: Money and Staffing

The marketing budget describes and allocates the resources needed to implement the strategies and actions contained in the marketing plan. Your company can benefit from the combination of the creative influence of the marketing plan and the logical discipline of the budgeting process.

In practice, many companies do not establish a marketing budget. There are many reasons for this. Professionals, such as accountants, attorneys, and physicians, have historically shunned promotions such as advertising. Even though standards of what is acceptable practice may change, it is difficult to alter the opinions of practitioners. Most of their marketing activities fall under entertainment or business and practice development.

Often business managers are not sure of what should be included in a marketing budget. Small business owners or managers may be uncertain of their income, and they often decide that any marketing activity will be too expensive. Many businesses of all sizes pay for marketing activities by default and without a particular plan. For example, when approached by customers or friends to sponsor ads in community publications or by sales representatives with interesting promotional ideas, they may act on what is presented without any coherent plan. The point is that, regardless of whether a company prepares a formal marketing budget, marketing activities happen.

Common Budget Practices

Companies can prepare marketing or expense budgets in various ways. Marketing budgets are commonly based on:

- Historical marketing, business development, or advertising expenses from prior years
- Industry averages for companies of similar size with similar product-service mixes
- Percentage of sales or anticipated sales
- The marketing plans for achieving sales and profit objectives that have been set for the budgeted year

The first method, basing the marketing budget on last year's expenses, has the benefit of assuring a minimum level of marketing support services for your company.

However, it does not acknowledge the fact that marketing needs may fluctuate from year to year.

The second practice, basing marketing budgets on industry averages, takes into account what your competition may be spending. It also provides a minimum level of marketing support services for your sales efforts. However, this method does not consider that you may be better at targeting your marketing efforts and may need more or less money for your marketing plan than the average.

Some companies allot a percentage of their sales or anticipated sales as the basis for constructing a marketing budget. This procedure ensures that the costs for marketing expenses, including promotion, will be covered by a specific number of sales, either actual or anticipated. This method treats marketing costs as variable. Like the other two methods, this method does not consider the fluctuating needs of your company nor the dynamics of your customer.

The fourth method of figuring a marketing budget begins with specific company objectives for profits and sales, develops marketing plans to achieve those objectives, and estimates specific costs to implement the strategies suggested in those marketing plans. Budgets are tailored to the needs of specific target markets for your products or services and the promotion necessary to reach those target markets. This method has become increasingly popular.

Why Prepare a Marketing Budget?

If marketing activities just happen anyway, why does a company need to prepare a marketing budget? Company managers who choose to prepare marketing or business development budgets expect results from their planning processes. They utilize marketing budgets for several reasons, including:

- Ensuring profit objectives
- Projecting cash flow needs
- Allocating manpower and other resources
- Anticipating their markets' cycles and needs
- Controlling market functions

What Is a Marketing Budget?

Marketing budgets are plans for marketing expenses to be incurred in the following year. They are known by a variety of names—professionals accurately call them business development budgets; business managers think of them as components of marketing planning; small business owners identify marketing activities as expenses; and company and marketing managers see them as tools that assist in moving the company from where it is now to where it wants to be in the future.

The marketing budget permits company managers to execute their marketing plans.

The Budgeting Process for Marketing Functions

A company's marketing budget is an integral part of its overall budget or financial plan and should be developed in conjunction with the other elements of the overall budget. Budgeting allows for allocation of human resources as well as financial resources.

In large companies that separate the financial management component from the marketing planning element, it is imperative that your two departments or divisions work together to project sales and cash flow forecasts. In small businesses without in-house financial managers, your accountant can help you prepare forecasts and budgets to accomplish your income goals.

Sales Forecasting

The various elements that go into developing a budget are interrelated. For example, budget development usually starts with preparation of the sales forecast and expected gross income. However, meeting the budgeted levels of sales and income likely depends on the marketing effort the company exerts, which, in turn, depends to a large extent on the size and effectiveness of the marketing budget and the promotions it funds.

To prepare a sales forecast you can utilize:

- Historical sales data of your company—its performance in prior years
- Industry averages for companies of similar size with similar product-service mixes
- The sales and profit objectives that have been set for the budgeted year

Because most companies offer more than one product or service, it is best to forecast sales by categories, such as by product or product line, service, department or division, or location, outlet, territory, or distribution channel. For example, if you choose to forecast by product categories, list your products and their performance in prior years. Apply your sales and profit objectives to each category as percents (a 15 percent increase in sales is calculated by multiplying previous sales by 1.15).

Just as you set maximum and minimum objectives for your marketing plans, you should establish a range for sales of each product. For example, you may decide that your minimum sales objective needs to be equal to the inflation rate of your area, e.g., 5 percent, while your maximum goal may be 15 percent. Note any anticipated trends, changes, or plans that may affect your projections in the coming year.

Planning Exercise 10-1.
Sales Forecasting

Date ____________ Sales Forecast for Company or Division ____________

List Products/Services Category*	*Prior Years Sales*		*Desired Change %*		*Projected Sales Range*
	199 _	*199 _*	*Min.*	*Max.*	
	$	$			$
1.					
2.					
3.					
4.					
5.					
TOTALS					

*This list may be categorized by product, product line, service, department or division, location, outlet, territory, or distribution channel, depending on your organization structure.

Expense Forecasting

Once you have a sales forecast, your budget should consider the cost of the marketing expenses necessary to achieve that sales forecast. As we discussed in the section on break-even analysis (see Chapter 7), expenses can be broken down into two broad categories: fixed or variable. Fixed costs include all costs incurred by your company without regard to the volume of production or sales, such as:

- Advertising
- Rent/Leasing
- Licenses
- Interest
- Administrative personnel costs
- Equipment
- Insurance
- Utilities

Variable costs are those that vary directly with each unit produced and/or sold. If you do not produce or sell anything, your variable costs are zero. Typically, variable costs include:

- Materials
- Production labor
- Packaging
- Some promotions
- Sales costs
- Commissions
- Delivery costs

The amount of money your company budgets for marketing activities must include both types of costs. These costs must be anticipated so that sufficient sales can be made to ensure that marketing and promotion costs and a reasonable profit are covered.

The marketing budget is handled as a subsegment of the total expense budget for your company (which includes costs for production, salaries, benefits for employees, payments for your building or office, and other operational [fixed and variable] expenses). It includes any costs related directly to the marketing functions of your company, such as research and promotional costs inherent in product packaging decisions. (The actual materials costs of packaging is included in the product production budget.)

Specific Marketing Functions

In this section, we list a number of marketing functions typically included in marketing budgets. It is not necessary to include all of these functions in your marketing budgets at any given time; consider only the ones that are appropriate for your company.

Several sections of the marketing budget are explained in more depth on the following pages, and sample budget outlines are provided. The budgets contain more examples than you would use at one time. This should help you project the total marketing costs for your proposed marketing plans.

Marketing Expenses—General Areas

1. Marketing research—Monitoring trends and opportunities
   Externally dictated factors
   Internally directed factors
2. Market research—Monitoring and special studies to describe markets and identify needs
3. Evaluation and planning—Processes to strengthen management decisions
4. Product-service expenses—Existing and new products-services modifications, extensions, or deletions
5. Pricing expenses—Existing and new products-services
6. Place-distribution expenses—Existing and new channels
7. Promotional expenses—ongoing and proposed
8. Training and motivational expenses—Marketing-related
9. Marketing staffing expenses—Full-time, temporary, contracted

As you select your company's strategies and marketing expenditures, you will combine the general area budgets into one comprehensive marketing budget. If you are a marketing manager in a company with several divisions or departments, you may have specific marketing functions or project tasks to budget. These specialized budgets will be combined with the other marketing managers' budgets to make up the total marketing budget for the company.

Marketing Research Expenses

Costs for this department or function in addition to general operating costs include the expenses of:

- Ongoing collection of information, such as monitoring trends, competition, and customer satisfaction
- Special market, product-service, or other project studies
- Additional staff necessary to collect or tabulate and analyze information in-house
- Professional research firm costs, as necessary

Examples of general operational costs for marketing research include:

- Space and staffing overhead
- Professional dues and fees
- Training costs
- Printing/publication costs
- Presentation expenses
- Postage/shipping fees
- Additional long-distance telephone charges
- Travel expenses
- Entertainment expenses

Ongoing research and information gathering in a small business might include only one or two of the functions listed, for a large corporation many functions may be included. (How to decide whether you should hire a research firm is discussed in Chapter 12.)

Ongoing market research activities include:

- Monitoring external environment
- Monitoring internal company factors
- New-customer surveys
- Cross-selling results
- Market share monitoring
- Information on competitors
- Market trends
- Closed account surveys
- Other continuous feedback obtained through internal records such as sales data and inventory turnover

Research and information gathering for existing products or services or the development of future products or services should be monitored through ongoing studies. However, most of this research is done on an as-needed basis and therefore falls into a special study category. For example, if figures show a sudden increase or decline in sales, it is helpful to be able to track the reasons, which can help company managers make decisions to either reduce the risk encountered or increase sales, perhaps by repeating a successful sales strategy. Special study marketing research may include activities such as describing and identifying markets, both current and potential; testing new or changed products or services; developing information on new techniques for manufacture or delivery of products or services; analyzing competition and its possible reactions to your plans; evaluating planning processes to strengthen management decisions; and initiating projects to help the company identify its markets and offer its goods or services to those markets.

Budget Example for Market Research

The owner of a local electrical contracting company wants information about the company's current customer base in order to develop a promotional plan for reaching other customers with similar needs. As a subcontractor, the company does initial electrical work for new construction as well as electrical work for individuals. Its two main markets are building contractors and residential accounts. The owner has decided to ask current customers for feedback on how services are being delivered and whether there is anything the company is not currently providing for its customers that would be desirable. The company has access to its customers' mailing addresses as well as their phone numbers. It already tracks how often its service is used both by the individuals and by the contractors.

Individuals will be contacted by telephone by trained part-time help. Those who are willing to respond will be sent a coupon for one free service call within a 35-mile radius, labor and parts not included. Businesses will be contacted directly by the owner.

The results of the survey will be compiled, tallied, and discussed with the manager and the technicians to identify changes to improve customer relations and to evaluate new ideas. An overall description of those individuals who responded will be developed; businesses will be categorized by other methods. Figure 10-1 is an example of a budget for this type of program.

Product-Service Expenses

Product-service expenses may be incurred in your marketing plans for both existing and new products-services as a result of new or expanded markets, product-service modifications, or changes in laws or channels of distribution. Responses to competitive moves, technological improvements, or corporate ownership changes may affect your product-service mix. Strategies that acknowledge product life cycle changes or positioning needs may also require funds.

Examples of product-service budget items include:

- Modifications, or extensions, or deletions
- Design and engineering for samples
- Style changes
- Color changes
- Quality ranges
- Warranty and liability requirements
- Added services
- Product life cycle actions
- Positioning options
- Packaging modifications
- Branding changes
- Label design and development

If your company organization includes product-service managers, all marketing expenses related to each manager's product-service are usually included in that manager's budget, as are operational costs for that department.

Figure 10-1. Marketing research sample budget.

FOR Home Care Electric Company

DATE July 11, 1993

EXPENSE CATEGORY	$BUDGET	$ACTUAL	$DIFFERENCE
Hourly wages for part-time phone help			
Training for those additional employees			
Development of questions to be asked			
Paper and time to copy questionnaires			
Time to collate and count responses			
Costs for free trips by technicians			
Lunches for business contacts by owner			
Time for evaluation and discussion by all,			
results and possible promotions to be			
included			
TOTAL EXPENSE	$	$	$
Total Sales Needed to Justify			

Budget Example for Product Extension

A paper mill is experimenting with two new standard colors for its copier paper. Its intention is to find out from a number of its most active accounts which new colors they would purchase in quantity if given the opportunity. Instead of a survey, the mill intends to offer the two new colors for a limited time on a trial basis and will monitor the reactions by the volume of orders received. See Figure 10-2 for the budget for this program.

Pricing Expenses

Pricing decisions affect the entire profit picture of your company. You cannot not stay in business by setting prices below costs or even at the break-even point. However, your basic marketing strategies may require adjustments to price in two areas: setting discount policies and establishing temporary reductions in price for existing or new products or services.

Criteria for offering discounts are generally built into your price structure. (See Chapter 7 for a fuller discussion of pricing.) The discount policies of your company are often the critical selling point for wholesale accounts; both the marketing manager and the financial manager should monitor profit margins closely to ensure that products or services are not sold at a loss.

Figure 10-3 is an example of a discount schedule for two types of toys in a product line. It demonstrates both quantity and payment discounts and gives no allowance for shipping. Any changes in the discount schedule that result from marketing decisions may require you to inform company sales representatives and wholesalers of the new structure. These changes may have been made to attract more wholesalers, to strengthen relationships with current wholesalers, or to encourage wholesalers to give price breaks to retailers.

Temporary adjustments to price may also require funds to implement, educate staff, promote, and monitor sales. Sometimes these funds are included in the promotion budget. However, financial management and marketing management should agree on pricing strategy; treating price as a separate element of the marketing budget encourages cooperative planning.

Price-related expenses may include setting or changing any of the following:

- Discounts and allowances
- Temporary reductions
- Coupons
- Introductory or anniversary offers
- Seasonal sales
- Temporary raises or add-ons
- Free or discounted services
- Estimates of demand behavior
- Contingency for competitive actions
- Negotiations and bargaining
- Licensing fees
- Sales and other taxes

Budget Example for Pricing

An anniversary for a regional event is approaching. It is the twenty-fifth anniversary of the great chili cook-off, and the planners would like to double the number of activities and increase the number of participants in attendance, as well as triple the

Figure 10-2. **Product-service sample budget.**

FOR Stanley Paper Company

DATE March 31, 1993

EXPENSE CATEGORY	$BUDGET	$ACTUAL	$DIFFERENCE
Brief customer phone survey			
to determine preferred colors			
Personnel to phone and analyze			
Dyes for new colors			
Time on machinery to produce trial run			
Possible costs of overruns if not sold			
Brochure explaining new colors available			
on limited basis			
New label design for packaging of new			
colors			
TOTAL EXPENSE	$	$	$
Total Sales Needed to Justify			

Figure 10-3. Wholesale price list, 1993.

Wholesale Discount:		TOY A	TOY B
Suggested Retail		$34.95	$6.95
6 to 24 cases	40%	20.97	4.17
25 to 48 cases	45%	19.22	3.82
49 to 108 cases	50%	17.48	3.48
109 cases and over	52%	16.78	3.34

Terms: Net 30 days (shipping and handling added to invoice). Cumulative discounts calculated quarterly.

number of spectators. They feel that the cook-off will draw more people with the added attractions. They would like to charge a minimal entrance fee for the spectators in order to help defray the costs to the city of staging the event. Figure 10-4 represents their expense budget.

Place-Distribution Expenses

Place or distribution expenses for existing and new channels, like all other aspects of marketing, are closely tied to your company's policies and resources and to the marketing strategies you choose. You are most likely to incur place or distribution expenses in connection with location choices and distribution channel selection and support.

Examples of marketing-related location expenses for your company include:

- Site selection research
- Area association dues or fees
- Signs
- Handling and shipping charges
- Additional staffing hours
- Security

Your clients or customers may incur expenses for coming to your location; you may choose to absorb or reimburse these costs as a marketing expense. Location choices are an important aspect of the customer's perceived value of your business, products, and services; therefore, their expectations of your business may change with location changes. Some location expenses are:

- Parking
- Bus or other transportation
- Return postage
- Delivery or shipping
- Sales tax

Distribution channels are the lifeline of your business. As noted in Chapter 8, which discussed distribution methods, these distribution channels and the people involved are not your employees; they need to be treated as you would any important target market. Expenses budgeted to support your wholesalers, dealers, sales representatives, retailers, or other outlets might include:

Figure 10-4. **Pricing sample budget.**

FOR Chili Cook-Off Silver Anniversary

DATE July 4, 1993

EXPENSE CATEGORY	$BUDGET	$ACTUAL	$DIFFERENCE
Costs for producing tickets			
Costs for collecting			
Added security			
Licensing fees			
TOTAL EXPENSE	$	$	$
Total Sales Needed to Justify			

- Evaluation and monitoring costs
- Product-service training
- Product-service materials
- Sales training
- Special discounts or allowances
- Trade area promotional support
- Delivery costs
- Special logistics
- Trade association dues and fees
- Entertainment and networking opportunities
- Delivery of samples or sales materials

Budget Example for Place-Distribution

The toy company that produces the Fuzzy Tail Rabbit has found that the demand for its product has far outdistanced its ability to produce the toy. Both its problem and its opportunity require finding a way to spread out the orders so that it can fill them over a period of time. It would like to maintain the new accounts that it has realized thanks to the popularity of the new toy without alienating any of its current customers. The company has decided to ship as many of the toys as possible to its current customers, along with statements promising to ship additional supplies free of shipping charge as soon as they become available. New accounts will receive a minimum order of two cases each and will be offered the same free shipping on future orders totaling one hundred units. The shipments will be accompanied by a notice that additional shipments will be available in three weeks. Figure 10-5 is the toy company's budget.

Promotional Expenses

Promotional expenses often make up the majority of the marketing manager's budgeted expenses. Because promotion can be very costly, it is imperative that your plan generate enough sales to cover your expenses as well as make a profit for the company. Promotion generally involves one or more of the following:

- Personal selling
- Direct mail
- Incentives
- Visuals
- Publicity and public relations
- Advertising

In this section, each element of promotion is presented separately, with descriptions of components and a sample budget. This allows similar types of promotions to be considered together; in a realistic promotion budget, you would want a mix of the elements described.

Personal Selling

Personal selling can be the most costly form of promotion because of the costs of time and the additional expenses of the salespeople. If the salaries and other staffing

Figure 10-5. Place-distribution sample budget.

FOR Nature's Pets Toy Company

DATE October 20, 1993

EXPENSE CATEGORY	$BUDGET	$ACTUAL	$DIFFERENCE
Cost of shipping to regular			
accounts			
Cost of shipping to new accounts—			
minimum orders			
Possibility of losing some regular			
customers and costs incurred			
Letters and postage to each customer			
Special training session for			
customer service reps and			
shipping personnel			
TOTAL EXPENSE	$	$	$
Total Sales Needed to Justify			

costs are built into the personnel or operational budget, the variable expenses that remain for personal selling may be included in the marketing budget for promotion.

Methods of personal selling include:

- Face-to-face sales calls
- Telephone contacts
- Special events
- Store contacts
- Telemarketing
- Trade shows
- Bazaars
- Mobile offices
- Showrooms

Expenses for personal selling may encompass:

- Commissions
- Travel
- Housing
- Meals
- Per diem expenses
- Entertainment and special events
- Long-distance telephone charges
- Trade show set-up and equipment
- Rental fees for tables, chairs, tents, etc.
- Shipping of samples and other materials
- Booth and entry fees for bazaars, fairs, contests
- Mobile offices
- Professional/technical memberships
- Seminars
- Lobbying expenses
- Printing and mailing fees

Budget Example for Personal Selling

A major pharmaceutical company plans to introduce a new headache remedy. Its main distribution is through its sales representatives. The company has invested a lot of money in research and development for this new product and would like to realize a return as soon as possible. Although it plans a full-scale promotional campaign, it would like to stock the stores in advance of this campaign. It will ask sales reps to talk with their accounts about the coming promotions and encourage them to have the product in stock ahead of time. See Figure 10-6 for the company's budget.

Direct Mail

Direct mail costs may be "hidden"—that is, not apparent at first glance. The most obvious expense is the cost of mailing or postage itself. U.S. postal service mail classifications include full first class, bulk first class, second class, bulk second class, and third class mail. In addition, there are other methods of delivering mail, such as fax, delivery service, U.S. Postal Express Mail service, UPS, and Federal Express. When preparing your budget, it pays to shop around.

In addition to the mailing costs, the costs of preparing the mailing piece must be considered. These expenses may be as low as three cents apiece for a copy machine flyer or as high as several thousand dollars for an original work of art with a note. Obviously, the marketing manager must be very specific about just what is to be mailed!

Methods of direct mail include:

- Brochures
- Letters
- Newsletters
- Media kits
- Catalogs
- Postcards
- Flyers
- Invitations
- Samples
- Overnight delivery services
- Fax

Figure 10-6. Personal selling sample budget.

FOR Savion Pharmaceutical

DATE November 13, 1993

EXPENSE CATEGORY	$BUDGET	$ACTUAL	$DIFFERENCE
Product and sales training			
for sales reps			
Brochures			
Order forms			
Additional travel expenses			
Additional commissions			
Long distance phone/Fax charges			
Samples			
TOTAL EXPENSE	$	$	$
Total Sales Needed to Justify			

Direct mail expenses may involve but are certainly not limited to the following:

- Design, production, and distribution of
    - brochures
    - letters
    - newsletters
    - media kits
    - catalogs
    - postcards
    - flyers
    - samples
    - invitations
- Envelopes
- Paper
- Mailing lists and labels—rentals or purchase
- Additional staff for addressing or other preparation
- Return reply charges

Budget Example for Direct Mail

A large regional office supply company has decided to sell overstocks of selected items by offering special prices. It plans to mail its customers a special order form that prices selected items at their wholesale cost (see Figure 10-7).

Incentives

An incentive may be a very small gift that costs a fraction of a cent or an expensive, large rebate. The cost of incentives varies widely. They are often used with other elements of promotion, increasing the expense.

Methods for providing incentives include:

- Gifts or specialties
- Purchase with a purchase
- Samples
- Coupons
- Rebates
- Awards
- Recognitions
- Rewards
- Contests

Some of the cost items to consider in your marketing budget if you choose to use incentives are:

- Gifts/specialties
- Product selection, design, and production for special purchases
- Sample design, production, and distribution costs
- Direct coupon or rebate costs, including retailer handling and postage costs
- Awards/recognitions development as well as costs of administration, record keeping, and special events
- Reward amounts and administration costs
- Contest development, judging, administration, and prizes
- Printing
- Possible packaging costs

Figure 10-7. **Direct mail sample budget.**

FOR East Coast Office Supply

DATE August 20, 1993

EXPENSE CATEGORY	$BUDGET	$ACTUAL	$DIFFERENCE
Printing of order form			
Postage			
Letter of introduction			
Labels			
Additional catalogs if requested			
TOTAL EXPENSE	$	$	$
Total Sales Needed to Justify			

Budget Example for Incentives

Chambers National Bank has seen a decline in the numbers of its regular savings accounts. It has decided to operate an instructional satellite "save-mobile" at the local elementary schools to offer young potential clients the opportunity to learn to open their own accounts. In addition, the students will receive information on savings programs and a coupon for $1 when they open their own accounts with a minimum balance of $25. Parents will need to assist the children in opening their accounts, either by mail or in person (see Figure 10-8).

Visuals

The visual elements of promotion create the presence and image that your company needs to be recognized by your current and potential markets. It is worth developing a comprehensive visual package, and the budget to produce it, for two reasons: (1) You do not change your visual identity very often, and (2) you can use these elements everywhere to promote a consistent image for your company.

Methods of using visuals include:

- Signs
- Business cards
- Stationery
- Billing statements
- All promotional materials
- Training materials
- Contracts
- Equipment
- Name tags
- Packaging
- Report covers
- Fax sheets

It is imperative that your marketing budget include the costs for the subsequent list of visuals, including the design and development of your company logo or distinctive typeface, business cards, and stationery products. Once these are developed, different departments place their orders and the costs go into your general operations budget.

In addition, your budget for use of visuals may encompass the costs of:

- Signs
- Forms, e.g., contracts, billing statements, fax sheets
- Report covers
- Brochures
- Packaging
- Name tags
- Training materials
- Company equipment, e.g., cars, trucks, musical instruments, briefcases, uniforms, linens
- Newsletters
- Clothing items, e.g., golf shirts, caps, jackets

Budget Example for Visuals

A consulting engineer has his own business. He has added a partner and wants to use this opportunity to change the company logo. They will need new business cards, stationery, and proposal covers (see Figure 10-9).

Figure 10-8. **Incentives sample budget.**

FOR Chambers National Bank

DATE September 12, 1993

EXPENSE CATEGORY	$BUDGET	$ACTUAL	$DIFFERENCE
Personnel to staff the "mobile"			
Rental of the "mobile"			
Flyer development and printing			
Coupon development and printing			
Costs of redeemed coupons,			
estimated on 7% return			
Phone calls to schools (time			
for personnel)			
Training of personnel, new accounts.			
TOTAL EXPENSE	$	$	$
Total Sales Needed to Justify			

Figure 10-9. Visual elements sample budget.

FOR Firm Foundation, Inc.

DATE November 30, 1993

EXPENSE CATEGORY	$BUDGET	$ACTUAL	$DIFFERENCE
Logo design			
Paper product designs			
Printing and material for:			
stationery			
envelopes			
business cards			
report covers			
TOTAL EXPENSE	$	$	$
Total Sales Needed to Justify			

Public Relations

Promotion through public relations (PR) or publicity can be a very economical way to enhance your promotional strategies and/or a very expensive way to promote your company and its products-services. In the sample budget below we present an economical PR strategy.

Methods of using publicity include:

- Print media
- Newspapers
- Magazines
- Trade journals
- Electronic media
- Television
- Radio
- Computer data banks
- Word-of-mouth
- Newsletters
- Grocery sacks
- Others' product packages
- Movies
- Newsreels/programs
- Plays
- Source leaks
- Events
- Games

Many other methods of publicity are open to your company. Publicity or public relations options are many and as unique as your imagination. The following list gives only some of the possible options and expenses. Who knows—your best friend may be a television talk show host!

Among the expenses associated with public relations are these:

- Development and production of media kits
- Audio and video expenses
- Copy writing costs
- Research for articles and features
- Publicist fees
- Professional association dues and fees
- Travel expenses
- Photography fees
- Entertainment expenses
- Printing costs
- Postage and delivery

Budget Example for Public Relations

A veterinarian invented a special product for use in grooming show horses. This product was available at specialty stores but did not meet anticipated sales because the vet could not afford to promote or advertise widely. In order to let groomers and horse owners know about the product, it was suggested that he obtain coverage in the national stock show magazine (see Figure 10-10).

Advertising

Advertising is probably the most common form of promotion used by all businesses. Although a company may not have a marketing budget, the general budget frequently has separate line items for your advertising budget. The costs of various vehicles for advertising vary greatly. It may be prudent to seek professional assistance either from a media buyer who purchases advertising space directly or from an

Figure 10-10. **Publicity and public relations sample budget.**

FOR Sam Steins, D.V.M.

DATE June 25, 1993

EXPENSE CATEGORY	$BUDGET	$ACTUAL	$DIFFERENCE
Independent PR person			
Phone calls			
Costs of photos			
Samples			
Mailing costs			
TOTAL EXPENSE	$	$	$
Total Sales Needed to Justify			

advertising agency or PR firm that purchases space in large quantities. Media rates can be obtained from the media sales representatives or from published data in the library. (Chapter 12 discusses research and information sources.)

Methods of using advertising include:

- Newspapers
- Radio
- Television
- Direct mail
- Cable TV
- Signs
- Trade journals
- Magazines
- Outdoor/transit
- Computer access
- Information service
- Coupon books
- Posters
- Banners
- Maps
- Events
- Books
- Airport booths
- Billboards
- Directories
- Movies
- Seminars

Advertising expenses may encompass but are not limited to these areas:

- Media space and/or time expenses
- Artwork design
- Camera-ready art in various sizes
- Photography (still and video)
- Concept development
- Copy writing
- Event sponsorship fees
- Telephone listings and ads
- Banner, flag design, and production
- Presentation materials
- Classified ad copy
- Advertising agency fees
- Printing
- Entertainment
- Professional fees and dues
- Research

Budget Example for Advertising

A realty company is starting a newcomer service to provide realtors with potential clients and give newcomers information about the area. Newcomers who respond to ads placed in selected magazines are sent current maps and a thirty-page booklet detailing facts and opportunities about the area (see Figure 10-11).

Figure 10-11. Advertising sample budget.

FOR Chateau Realty

DATE April 15, 1994

EXPENSE CATEGORY	$BUDGET	$ACTUAL	$DIFFERENCE
Agency fee for:			
ad design art			
ad copy			
ad space costs			
Development of booklet			
Costs of maps			
Postage			
Training of realtors			
TOTAL EXPENSE	$	$	$
Total Sales Needed to Justify			

Planning Exercise 10-2.
Sample Marketing Budget Worksheet

This sample budget form may be used for developing any of your marketing budgets. Transfer the totals on all your budget worksheets to Strategic Playsheet 14, Marketing Budget.

SAMPLE BUDGET—EXPENSES

FOR

DATE

EXPENSE CATEGORY	$BUDGET	$ACTUAL	$DIFFERENCE
TOTAL EXPENSE	$	$	$
Total Sales Needed to Justify			

Putting the Company Marketing Budget Together

After the sales and income forecasts are completed and the costs or expenses for marketing strategies are compiled, the marketing components and their associated costs need to be summarized and presented to management for approval. All marketing plans should include marketing budgets; the two are usually approved at the same time.

In large companies and especially in tight economic times, don't be surprised if you are asked to cut your activities and expenses. The marketing function is a serious and valuable asset for any business; however, because it is more flexible than other business functions, such as finance and production, marketing managers are often asked to develop alternative strategies. This may be frustrating, but developing creative alternatives is part of your position—and your challenge. There are many combinations of plans and budgets that will achieve your stated company profit goals and objectives. As you develop your initial marketing plans and budgets, keep in mind contingency options for alternative actions.

When the marketing expenses are summarized in the overall company expense budget, the line items may look like Strategic Playsheet 14.

STRATEGIC PLAYSHEET 14.

Marketing Budget (date ____________)

Marketing functions typically associated with budgeting needs are listed here. Check the functions which are appropriate for your company to include in its Marketing Budget.

Company Name
1993 Profit Plan—Projected Expenses

	First Quarter	*Second Quarter*	*Third Quarter*	*Fourth Quarter*	*TOTAL*
MARKETING EXPENSE					
Marketing research					
Market development					
Product-service					
Pricing					
Licenses and taxes					
Distribution					
Promotions					
Advertising					
Public relations					
Personal selling					
Direct mail					
Incentives					
Visuals					
Personnel, Marketing					
Salaries					
Benefits					
Commissions					
Temporary assistant					
Training					
Legal and Professional					
Legal					
CPA–accounting					
Research firm					
Ad agency					
PR firm					
Artist					
Copy writer					
Membership dues					

	First Quarter	*Second Quarter*	*Third Quarter*	*Fourth Quarter*	*TOTAL*
Administrative					
Office space					
Supplies					
Postage/freight					
Insurance					
Utilities					
Printing					
Travel					
Entertainment					
Internal communications					
Telephone					
Fax					
Storage					
TOTAL					

Strategy Check for Budget and Evaluation

1. Name your target markets: ______________________________

____

____

____

2. On the basis of the products and services, price ranges, distribution methods, and promotions strategy you have selected for these markets, what marketing budget do you need?

____

What additional resources, such as personnel, facilities, and research, will you need?

____

____

____

3. Who needs to approve this budget? ______________________________
What, if any, additional steps need to be taken? ______________________________

____

____

4. Will this strategy work within the limitations you identified earlier?

EXTERNALLY LIMITING FACTORS:

Political and legal environment	Yes	No
Cultural and social environment	Yes	No
Economic environment	Yes	No
Technological environment	Yes	No
Competitive environment	Yes	No
Industrial environment	Yes	No

INTERNALLY DIRECTED FACTORS:

Goals and objectives	Yes	No
Ethics	Yes	No
Internal resources	Yes	No

5. State the objective this strategy will help to fulfill. ______________________________

____

____

____

6. What does success look like for this marketing plan? ______________________________

____

____

____

____

The Creative Solutions: Your Marketing Plan

11

Writing Your Marketing Plan

Marketing plans may be written for specific products, services, markets, projects, or divisions. Generally, several marketing plans are developed for various products or services of the company; those plans are then combined to form a master marketing plan. When developing your master marketing plan, remember to target several large markets with overlapping needs; these tend to be the most profitable.

Marketing plans are usually developed at the same time the yearly budgeting process is undertaken so that adequate funds for marketing can be allocated. (For a detailed discussion of marketing budget development, see Chapter 10.)

Although marketing plans are put together once a year, they should incorporate built-in review dates, at which times their success will be evaluated. Such reviews often take place after six months, at the completion of a phase or cycle, or when any necessary modifications are made. Sometimes, a special plan is developed during the year for a short-term project; its timetable is independent of that for the overall marketing plan.

As a general guideline, the person who will be responsible for implementing the marketing plan should write it. This person can be the company owner or marketing manager, a project coordinator, a product manager, or a salesperson.

Putting Your Plan on Paper

Most business managers and marketing professionals have a good working knowledge of the principles of marketing. However, writing a marketing plan in a clear, concise manner can be quite trying. This chapter includes several different formats for you to try out as you write, see, and discuss your marketing plans. The outlines and forms presented here will help you and those responsible for marketing planning put your plans on paper.

On the following pages, you will find five alternative ways to create your marketing plan.

1. A collection of fourteen Strategic Playsheets which together form a framework for your initial marketing plan, including budgets. These playsheets are identical to those that have appeared throughout this book.
2. A Short Form that summarizes the external factors and the company elements that have been identified in the Strategic Playsheets. The columns represent target markets and the adjustable 4 Ps (product-service, price, place-distribution, and promotion) of your marketing mix. This form can be used to

encourage group discussion of your options. It may be copied from the book and distributed to those involved in developing your plan, or you may use overheads or flip charts to project it on the wall for discussion.

3. A Basic Outline that serves as a checklist for writing your marketing plans, either in outline or paragraph form. Its order helps you to present good written reports.
4. A Marketing Plan Time Line and Responsibility chart, helpful for assigning responsibilities and managing the implementation of your marketing plan. This chart helps the marketing manager record specific activities, the person(s) responsible for them, and the estimated time needed to accomplish them. The Marketing Plan Time Line and Responsibility chart helps you control and monitor the tasks of your marketing plans.
5. A Marketing Audit outline that provides a detailed list of marketing areas for planning. The outline serves as a guide for marketing situation analyses, which can serve as periodic benchmark studies, help you to evaluate past strategies, identify problem areas and possible strategies for handling them. The Marketing Audit, which is usually written in paragraph form with accompanying charts and tables, can help you to define your parameters and options whenever you accept a new marketing position, introduce a new product or service, or plan to enter a major new market.

In the remainder of this chapter, we discuss each method of writing your marketing plan and provide the appropriate forms.

Strategic Playsheets

In each chapter of this book, you made strategic marketing choices and recorded them on fourteen Strategic Playsheets, which together form a framework for your initial marketing plans, including budgets. Copies of the Strategic Playsheets are provided on the following pages.

STRATEGIC PLAYSHEET 1.

Cover Page

MARKETING PLAN
for

Company name: ______________________________

prepared by

Name, title: ______________________________

Date: ______________________________

approved by

Name, title: ______________________________

Date: ______________________________

Review date: ______________________________

STRATEGIC PLAYSHEET 2.

Vision Statement

Now, rewrite your vision in one or two sentences in the space below. Remember that you want to provide a future-focused guide for today's actions.

Vision Statement ____

____

____

____

Refined Vision Statement for ____________________ Company ____________________

____

____

____

STRATEGIC PLAYSHEET 3.

History and Goals for ______________ Company

Fill in a summary of your company's history here. ______________________________

____

____

____

____

____

____

____

____

Fill in your goals and objectives here. Use only the major marketing goals that were checked in Chapter 1.

1. ____
____
2. ____
____
3. ____
____
4. ____
____

STRATEGIC PLAYSHEET 4.

Distinctive Advantage for ____________________ Company

A distinctive advantage is a unique area of excellence that your company has and that it may use to its advantage.

On the basis of the analysis of your internal resources, list the distinctive advantages of your company.

Manpower ____

Money ____

Time ____

Materials ____

STRATEGIC PLAYSHEET 5.

Rationale for Marketing Plan for ____________________ Company

Write a sentence or two that explains what brought you to develop this plan: __________

STRATEGIC PLAYSHEET 6.

Strategic Options for _________________ Company
Analysis of Competition

The product under consideration for this plan is ______________. In this product area, we are a _________-sized company. Listed below are our strategic options, our major competitors, and their anticipated reaction to each of our strategic options.

SPECIFIC STRATEGIC OPTIONS	COMPETITORS	ANTICIPATED REACTIONS
1.		
2.		
3.		
4.		
5.		

From a competitive standpoint, which option appears to be most in your company's favor? Circle it.

STRATEGIC PLAYSHEET 7.

Environmental Situation Summary for ________________ Company

Briefly summarize your areas of distinctive advantage. State what you have learned about your competition that will influence this plan. Specifically, which windows of opportunity will you seek to fill with this plan? What external factors affect this plan? What internal factors affect this plan? ____

STRATEGIC PLAYSHEET 8.

Setting Marketing Objectives for ____________________ Company

Rewrite the two marketing goals for your company that you identified in Chapter 1. List a maximum and a minimum marketing objective that will move your company toward each goal.

GOAL 1 ____

____

[Each goal may require one or more specific actions. Those actions are objectives. Write both minimum and maximum objectives for goals. By setting these expectations, you will have a broader range within which to achieve success.]

OBJECTIVES	DATE	
	Minimum	Maximum
What is to be achieved?		
By when?		
By whom?		
How will it be measured?		

GOAL 2 ____

____

____

OBJECTIVES	DATE	
	Minimum	Maximum
What is to be achieved?		
By when?		
By whom?		
How will it be measured?		

STRATEGIC PLAYSHEET 9.

Description of Target Markets by Facts and Needs

If you think a target market wants or needs your products and services, re-analyze the actual needs of that market(s) here.

DESCRIPTION OF TARGET MARKET

Target Market Name: ____________________

Description of Facts | Description of Needs

Description of Target Markets by Facts and Needs

Mass market or single target market

Overlapping target markets

If you can't find a "need" match to your company, either change markets or modify products, whichever is cheaper. Selection of the appropriate target market(s) is the most important adjustable factor in your marketing strategy mix. Identifying their NEEDS correctly is the second most important task in marketing planning.

STRATEGIC PLAYSHEET 10.

Matching Product-Service Mix to Target Markets

MARKETING OBJECTIVE ______________________________

____

TARGET MARKET ______________________________

COMPANY'S PERCEPTION OF PRODUCT OR SERVICE

Target Market Description	Product-Service Features
______________	______________
______________	______________
______________	______________
______________	______________
______________	______________
______________	______________

CUSTOMER'S PERCEPTION OF PRODUCT OR SERVICE

Target Market Needs	Product-Service Benefits
______________	______________
______________	______________
______________	______________
______________	______________
______________	______________
______________	______________

STRATEGIC PLAYSHEET 11.

Determining Price for ________________ Company

1. Estimate the demand by looking closely at your target markets. You can use past sales of similar products—yours, the industry's, or your competitors'. What do you estimate the demand for your products to be? ________________

2. Look at your competition chart in Chapter 3. Is there a price leader, one company that appears to be #1? ________ If so, are your prices in line with those of similar products? ________ Are territories a factor? ________ What are the general discount policies within your industry? ________

   What are the possible and probable reactions of your competitors to your pricing? ________

3. In view of the target market's needs and the strength and number of competitors in your field, what is your current market share? ______ What do you expect this plan to do to that market share? ________

4. Look at your pricing strategy options in light of your company objectives for using the product life cycle. Are your products spread over all phases of the product life cycle, or are they bunched in one sector? What does this tell you? ________

5. What is the price range that you determined in this chapter? ________

   What is your break-even price? ________
   Is there an opportunity to maintain perceived value of your products and cut costs? How? ________

6. Select a pricing strategy: low prices/high volume or high prices/low volume. Compare your strategy with your objectives and the resources of your company; with the legal limitations or opportunities; with pricing ranges currently offered; and with the product-service offering of your company. State your strategy. ________

7. Seek advice from your accountants and your sales people before setting a final price policy.
   Anticipated suggested retail price range: ______________________________
   ____
   ____
   Anticipated wholesale discount percentage: ______________________________

8. Monitor your sales, profits, and competitor reactions closely. Adjust if needed, but not frequently.

STRATEGIC PLAYSHEET 12.

Selecting Distribution Methods for ______________Company

Review this list of questions before settling on the appropriate place to sell your products and services.

1. Market Considerations
   As you did with the other two Ps, product and price, start with your target markets.
   Where are they located? ______________________________
   How can you most easily get your products and/or services to them?
   ____
   Are several territories involved or only one? ______________________________
   What is the potential number of customers? ______________________________
   What is their usual order size? ______________________________
   Who buys your products and services? ______________________________
   ____
   How often do they buy them? ______________________________
   Why do they buy them? ______________________________

2. Product-Service Considerations
   What marketing logistics are required to handle the product or service?
   ____
   Is it perishable? Or does it have a long shelf-life? ______________________________
   Is it technical in nature, requiring specialized installation or explanation?
   ____
   What is its size? Is it large and bulky or neatly packaged, a dozen to a box?
   ____
   Is mail a consideration? ________ How much does it weigh? ______________________________

3. Company Considerations
   What are your goals and objectives for this product or service?
   ____
   What services are you willing to offer?
   ____
   Are you limited to one location? ______________________________
   How much control over distribution do you seek? Do you want the product to be uniquely available through your sales force, or do you want it widely available through various outlets or methods? ______________________________
   ____
   Where are you located in relation to your target market? ______________________________
   ____
   Does another middleman have better access to that market? ______________________________
   Are there legal or cultural issues to consider? ______________________________

4. Make your distribution choices here. Try to think of at least two different ways in which you could profitably get your products or services to your selected target market.

1. ______________________ 3. ______________________

2. ______________________ 4. ______________________

____

STRATEGIC PLAYSHEET 13.

Promotion Selection Process for ______________________ Company

Consider the following questions BEFORE you develop your message:

1. Place the name of the target markets here:

____

____

2. What are the common needs of your target markets?

____

____

3. What benefits satisfy those needs?

____

____

4. What specific objectives are you seeking? What do you want the target markets to do?

____

____

5. What are the most direct routes for communicating with your target markets? Choose your elements of promotion here:

____

____

____

6. In fifteen words or less, write your message here:

____

____

7. List any feedback you have from the current promotion here:

____

____

____

____

At this point you may decide to start all over or you may decide to go on to other markets or another promotion strategy for these markets.

____

STRATEGIC PLAYSHEET 14.

Marketing Budget (date ___________)

Marketing functions typically associated with budgeting needs are listed here. Check the functions which are appropriate for your company to include in its Marketing Budget.

Company Name
1993 Profit Plan—Projected Expenses

	First Quarter	*Second Quarter*	*Third Quarter*	*Fourth Quarter*	*TOTAL*
MARKETING EXPENSE					
Marketing research					
Market development					
Product-service					
Pricing					
Licenses and taxes					
Distribution					
Promotions					
Advertising					
Public relations					
Personal selling					
Direct mail					
Incentives					
Visuals					
Personnel, Marketing					
Salaries					
Benefits					
Commissions					
Temporary assistant					
Training					
Legal and Professional					
Legal					
CPA–accounting					
Research firm					
Ad agency					
PR firm					
Artist					
Copy writer					
Membership dues					

	First Quarter	*Second Quarter*	*Third Quarter*	*Fourth Quarter*	TOTAL
Administrative					
Office space					
Supplies					
Postage/freight					
Insurance					
Utilities					
Printing					
Travel					
Entertainment					
Internal communications					
Telephone					
Fax					
Storage					
TOTAL					

The Short Form

The Short Form summarizes in paragraph form the external factors and company elements that you identified on Strategic Playsheets 1 through 8 and in columns the information from Strategic Playsheets 9 through 14. Each column is numbered and titled to correspond to a specific playsheet. This form can be used to encourage group discussion of marketing options. If you discover that you need more information as you discuss these options, place a star next to those items that require further research.

THE SHORT FORM: MARKETING STRATEGY PLAYSHEET SUMMARY

1. Cover Sheet ____________________

2. Vision ____________________

3. History and Goals ____________________

4. Distinctive Advantages ____________________

5. Rationale ______________________________

6. Strategy Options ______________________________

7. Summary External Factors ______________________________

8. Marketing Objectives ______________________________

Maximum 1. ______________________________

2. ______________________________

Minimum 1. ______________________________

2. ______________________________

MARKETING STRATEGY SUMMARY—PLAYSHEETS 9 THROUGH 14

	9 *Market Selected*	9 *Description Facts*	9 *Needs*	10 *Product Features*	10 *Product Benefits*	11 *Price*
1.						
2.						
3.						

MARKETING STRATEGY SUMMARY—PLAYSHEETS 9 THROUGH 14

12 Place Distribution	*13 Promotion*	*13 Message*	*14 Marketing Budget*	*Evaluation & Feedback*
1.				OBJECTIVES MET Maximum: Minimum: Feedback for future planning:
2.				OBJECTIVES MET Maximum: Minimum: Feedback for future planning:
3.				OBJECTIVES MET Maximum: Minimum: Feedback for future planning:

The Basic Outline

The Basic Outline serves as a checklist for writing your marketing plans, either in outline or short paragraph form. This outline, accompanied by brief notes describing the actions needed, can be used for your marketing plan. It works well when the terminology used is generally known within the company and when one or two people are directing the implementation. Next to using the Summary of Strategic Playsheets, this outline is the simplest report to write because it requires only very brief statements for each section. Most project managers and entrepreneurs find this type of marketing plan useful.

Many marketing managers have found that, when a great number of people will be referring to the marketing plan, an outline with more detailed text under each heading is necessary. Remember that the marketing plan is a working, communication tool; select the form that you believe fits your organization.

Basic Outline for Marketing Plans

MARKETING PLAN FOR ______________

Developed by ________________________

Date ______________________________

I. INTRODUCTION—A brief statement of background information about the company, the rationale that led to this plan, and the specific maximum and minimum objectives of this plan.

II. MARKET IDENTIFICATION—A brief description of the target market(s) and the common needs this plan will serve.

III. COMPETITION—An evaluation of how the competition serves (or does not serve) this market and how the competition may react to your plans.

IV. STRATEGY FOR EACH TARGET MARKET
  - A. Brief summary of strategy
  - B. Marketing mix factors—adjustables
    - 1. Product-service mix
      - a. Lines and quality
      - b. Brands and image
      - c. Packaging
      - d. Services
      - e. Product life cycle
      - f. Miscellaneous
    - 2. Price mix
      - a. Basic price, discounts, allowances
      - b. Credit available
      - c. Transportation and shipping
      - d. Grants and loans

e. Implicit costs
f. Miscellaneous
3. Place-distribution mix
a. Location
b. Territories
c. Marketing logistics
d. Miscellaneous
4. Promotion mix
a. Publicity
b. Sales promotions
c. Personal selling
d. Advertising
e. Incentives
f. Miscellaneous

C. Action plans
1. Specific tasks
2. Time line for completion
3. Budget
4. Assignment of tasks and authority

D. Measurement guidelines and review dates (criteria for success)
1. Achieving objectives stated in (Introduction).
2. Solving target market needs X, Y, or Z.
3. Increasing customers/sales by X percent.
4. Contributing to the attainment of the company's goals.

V. ESTIMATED SCHEDULE (TIME LINE)
(See below)

VI. MARKETING BUDGET

VII. NOTES, COMMENTS, SOURCES (if needed)

Note: This format can be used for general marketing programs, e.g., those with companywide impact, and for specific division, industry, product, service, or project plans.

MARKETING FUNCTIONS AND TIME LINE SCHEDULE

		Estimated Planned Schedule			*Actual Schedule*	
		Time	*Dates*		*Dates*	
Function	*Responsibility*	*Required*	*Start*	*Finish*	*Start*	*Finish*

The Marketing Plan Time Line and Responsibility Chart

The Marketing Plan Time Line and Responsibility Chart is a quick method for doing small-project plans. It is also helpful for assigning responsibilities and managing the implementation of your marketing plan. This chart helps the marketing manager note specific activities, the person(s) responsible for them, and the estimated time needed to accomplish them. Budget data may be included here or presented separately. However, as always, it is important to relate your expenses to your marketing plan.

MARKETING PLAN FOR ______________
DEVELOPED BY ______________
DATE ______________

MARKETING PLAN TIME LINE AND RESPONSIBILITIES OUTLINE AND CHART

		*Estimated Schedule**		*Actual Schedule**		
Functions	*Responsibility*	*Start*	*Finish*	*Start*	*Finish*	*Budget*
Introduction						
Background of Company						
Strengths/ weaknesses						
Specific objectives						
Maximum/ minimum						
1. What is to be achieved?						
2. By when?						
3. By whom?						
4. How measured?						
Competition						
Strengths/ weaknesses						
Evaluation & research						
Rationale						
Market Identification						
Target market description						
Target market needs						

Functions	*Responsibility*	*Estimated Schedule** *Start*	*Finish*	*Actual Schedule** *Start*	*Finish*	*Budget*
Product-Service Mix						
Lines and quality						
Brands and image						
Packaging						
Added services						
Product life cycle						
Price Mix						
Basic price						
Discounts						
Credit						
Transportation						
Grants and loans						
Risks						
Place-Distribution Mix						
Location						
Territories						
Logistics						
Promotion Mix						
Publicity						
Sales promotion						
Personal selling						
Advertising						
Incentives						
Strategy Summary						
Measurement Plans						
Specific objectives						
Maximum/ minimum						
1. What is to be achieved?						
2. By when?						
3. By whom?						
4. How measured?						

*Time required, e.g., 1 hour, 2 days, or 1 week

The Marketing Audit

The Marketing Audit outline, which provides a detailed list of marketing areas for planning, serves as a guide for a marketing situation analysis. Whenever you accept a new marketing position, introduce a new product or service, or plan to enter a major new market, a marketing audit can help you to define your parameters and options. This information is gathered to establish a benchmark and is reviewed before a high-risk major strategy is selected and implemented. It is not necessary to accumulate this information every year.

The marketing audit is usually written in paragraph form, with accompanying charts and tables. A sample report format follows.

Marketing Audit or Situation Analysis

Title page
Table of contents
List of tables
List of figures
Executive summary
Body of report
Appendixes
Bibliography

MARKETING AUDIT
FOR ______________________________
DATE ______________________________

Body of Report

I. Introduction
   A. Vision statement
   B. Brief background of company
   C. Goals
   D. Strengths and weaknesses

II. Limiting factors—Externally dictated factors
   A. Political and legal environment
      1. Laws
      2. Licenses
      3. Company structure
      4. Opportunities and limitations
   B. Cultural and social environment
      1. Business climate
      2. Expectations of community
      3. Other

- C. Economic environment
  1. Trends and forecasts
  2. Opportunities
- D. Technological environment
  1. Trends and innovations
  2. Opportunities
- E. Competitive environment
  1. Identities
  2. Products, prices, distribution, promotion
  3. Strengths and weaknesses
- F. Industrial environment
  1. Trends and forecast
  2. Opportunities
  3. Image and ethics
  4. Coalitions

III. Limiting Factors—Internally Dictated Factors
- A. Manpower, finances, facilities and equipment, materials, image, reputation
- B. Personal and corporate ethics
- C. Strengths and weaknesses

IV. Adjustable Opportunities: Market Profile (Customer Analysis)
- A. Major target markets
  1. Consumers
  2. Businesses and organizations
- B. Characteristics
  1. Demographics
  2. Sociographics
  3. Psychographics
- C. Trends

V. Adjustable Opportunities: Marketing Mix
- A. Product-service mix analysis
  1. Lines and quality
  2. Brands
  3. Packaging
  4. Services
  5. Product life cycle analysis
- B. Pricing mix analysis
  1. Basic price, discounts
  2. Credit available
  3. Transportation and shipping
  4. Grants and loans
  5. Implicit costs, time, and risk
- C. Place-distribution mix analysis
  1. Locations
  2. Territories
  3. Marketing logistics

D. Promotion mix analysis
   1. Publicity
   2. Sales promotion
   3. Personal selling
   4. Incentives
   5. Advertising
   6. Other

VI. Company's Marketing Objectives and Strategies
   A. Maximum and minimum objectives
   B. Summary of strategies

VII. Measurement: Historical Performance Comparisons
   A. General performance over past 3 to 5 years
   B. Current position vs. industry
   C. Current position vs. previous year's objectives
   D. Current position vs. industry forecasts
   E. Sales data (dollars and units) trends
   F. Market share data trends
   G. Marketing budget comparisons
   H. Other company measurements

VIII. Summary and Conclusions

IX. The Marketing Plan: Creative Solutions and Recommendations

X. Marketing Budget

Information Resources

12

Marketing Research and Information Gathering

As you prepare a marketing plan or evaluate your options for future actions, you may find that you do not have all the information you need and that further marketing research is required.

A technical definition of marketing research includes the systematic, objective gathering, recording, and analyzing of data concerning the problems and opportunities that confront management as it strives to serve markets profitably. Throughout this book, we have suggested ways to obtain information that you may need. In this chapter we present some basic information about marketing research as a tool and how to use it.

Why Does a Business Need Research?

Business managers use marketing research to monitor and understand their external and internal environments so that they may recognize opportunities to serve their customers profitably. Research assists marketing decision makers by identifying, characterizing, and segmenting target markets and provides a bridge for matching the needs of your customers or potential customers with the appropriate benefits of your products and services.

You may find it useful to think about marketing research as either information gathered on an ongoing basis (customer comments, sales data, closed account trends, sales representatives notes) or information gathered for special purposes (decisions on product modifications, new market descriptions, advertising tests). Some of the more common research requirements for marketing planning include:

- Understanding and monitoring your company's current position and trends regarding its external situation and internal environment.
- Learning about your business and consumer markets and their needs. Typically, research focuses on demographics (How accessible are the members of these markets? Who are they? Where are they? What do they want and need?); income patterns; and buying habits (Are they willing to spend their money? What factors influence their decisions?).
- Discovering information that will help you adjust your 4 Ps to serve your markets.

Sample Information Needs of Businesses

The information needs of businesses touch on every aspect of their internal and external environments. Up-to-the-minute data on the company, on its competitors, and on the external business situation are essential if you are to be in a position to identify those windows of opportunity on which your company's profitability may depend.

Political and Legal Aspects

- Your business environment can be expanded or limited by the political and legal climate of your city, region, or state. Keep in close contact with your trade association and/or your chamber of commerce, which monitor and lobby issues on your behalf.

Cultural and Social Expectations

- These change slowly. Recent business trends include a move toward more socially and ecologically responsible practices.
- Support "causes" that match your business goals for mutual benefits.
- When entering a new territory or market, learn its particular mores and customs.

Economic Factors

- Note any shift that directly affects your suppliers, distributors, or financial resources.
- Watch for changes that affect consumers of your products and services.
- Seek opportunities to turn negatives into positives for your company and its customers.

Competition and Technological Developments

- Who?
- What?
- Where?
- How successful?

Industrial Trends

- Note general factors that may affect your specific business, e.g., takeovers, mergers, closures.
- Watch for any changes in supply industries.
- Identify possibly beneficial coalitions.

Company Internal Resources and Objectives

- Money available
- People
- Business cycles
- Materials and equipment
- Company vision

- Yearly plan
- Marketing goals

Ethical Environment

- Your business code of ethics should be in alignment with your personal values.
- Without ethical standards for accountability, marketing processes can become manipulative.

Types of Research

There is literally no end to the amount of research you may gather. There is no substitute for research, but it can be distracting if you don't have a clear-cut use in mind. In fact, some managers nearly paralyze their decision making by requiring volumes of information before taking any action. Data should help you consider and evaluate options that move your business forward; information should be used as a tool, not as a crutch.

Secondary Research

Most business information needs can be satisfied by using sources that are already available (secondary data). Secondary research studies use information that was gathered for another purpose but that can help define the problem, identify the trend, or answer your current question. Always search secondary research sources before you launch an elaborate research project; many times you can either fully answer your questions or narrow the scope of your problem by reviewing the existing research.

A representative list of marketing research sources and where to find them is provided in the Sources of Information section. The following brief list suggests a variety of easily accessible places where you can begin to gather data for your marketing plans.

- *Your Company's Internal Records.* These provide ongoing information about your company through annual reports; sales data (by markets, products, divisions, etc.); ongoing surveys of customers (new, current, closed accounts); sales representatives feedback; oral and written company history; newspaper clipping file; thank-you notes from customers, suppliers, and community organizations.
- *Community Sources.* These offer trend and economic data for your area. Possible sources are the local chamber of commerce, local or regional trade associations, newspaper offices, banks or other financial institutions, political representatives' offices, police departments, insurance companies, local media, and nonprofit organizations (United Way, hospitals, resource centers, museums, libraries, etc.).
- *Academic Sources.* These offer a wide range of resources. In this category are public and private school systems, local and state colleges and universities, specialized research groups, and individual professors, doctors, teachers, and consultants.
- *Published Sources.* These include local libraries, government publications (census, statistical information for state and local areas), trade association libraries, trade publication statistical issues, and telephone books.

Primary Research

If your secondary research cannot answer the questions you have or if the decisions you must make for your business involve great risks in terms of time, money, potential income, or image, then you should consider using primary research—studies in which the data are collected for the specific problem(s) at hand. Some techniques for gathering primary data are:

- Observation—structured recordings
- Focus groups—small group discussions moderated by a skilled research interviewer
- Experiments—trials and comparisons
- Surveys—structured questions asked through mail, telephone, personal interview, or electronic means
- Test markets—introduction of product or service in limited area and/or with limited markets

Business problems usually require analysis of secondary research sources and, sometimes, one or more primary studies. When your risks in money, time, and/or image are very high, research becomes even more important.

Understanding Research

The ability to synthesize, interpret, and write a synopsis of your research is invaluable. Understanding the information available to your business is much more important than having file cabinets full of research that is never reviewed. Many studies can be done in-house; most studies should be directed by the person or group responsible for marketing planning.

Understanding the purpose of your study facilitates the choice of methods. *Exploratory purpose* research is flexible research that can be used to explore options, further define your needs, or for the following reasons:

- To discover ideas and insights
- To identify problems
- To establish priorities
- To clarify concepts
- To bring company personnel to a consensus

Conclusive purpose research, on the other hand, is rigid and uses scientific methods. Your company may use conclusive research to:

- Describe characteristics of certain groups or markets
- Estimate behavior patterns
- Make specific predictions
- Attempt to describe cause and effect relationships

When Should You Call in the Experts?

You can usually gather, review, and interpret ongoing data reports in-house with minimum expense. Special purpose data can be gathered in-house if you have the time and expertise to define your problems adequately, select your sample sources, and design and interpret the information. However, when the risks in terms of time, money, and image are very high, it is better to seek the advice of marketing research professionals.

As you assess your information needs, consider the following questions:

1. ***What can you do yourself or in-house?***

- Customer profiles
- Analysis of sales and services to customers
- Analysis of cross-selling or repeat sales
- Employee sales performance
- Identification and evaluation of competition
- Analysis of other company data
- Survey of secondary data
- Most exploratory research

2. ***When should you seek help?***

- Problem not easily defined
- High-risk situations
- Limited "in-house" expertise or time for research
- Information time line critical
- Outside "authority" needed
- Objective, scientific report critical
- Most conclusive research

3. ***How do you select a research firm?***

- Chamber of Commerce (or similar organization) membership directory
- American Marketing Association International Membership Directory and Marketing Services Guide
- Referrals from other business managers who have contracted for marketing research
- Interviews with representatives of research firms

Interviewing Representatives of Marketing Research Firms

There are a number of important areas you should cover when you meet with marketing researchers. The following outline suggests some of the most frequently asked questions.

Project execution data

- What are the steps or procedures they intend to use in this study? Why?
- What quality controls will they employ at each step?
- What statistical procedures are needed? Make sure they can explain them in a manner that will make the information useful for your company.
- What verification procedures will be used?

Key Individual Data

- Specifically who (names) will design, supervise, and conduct your research? What are their backgrounds and special qualifications?
- Can they analyze and synthesize data so that the information is useful to you and to your business planning?
- Do they have solid references?
- What is the amount of time key individuals will actually spend on your project?
- Have you met all of the key individuals who will work on your project?

Firm Background

- What are the firm's total personnel resources?
- What are its computer and tabulation resources?
- Do you want other references?

Costs

- What is the bid for the total cost of your project?
- What is the cost breakdown? You may want to conduct some of the steps in-house; many product or marketing managers prefer to interpret the data and write up the results for presentation to management themselves.
- What, if any, expenses will you incur (e.g., long-distance calls, report preparation costs, or follow-up fees) in addition to the above project costs? Because response rates and condensed time lines may cause extra expenses, it is common for research firms to include a plus-or-minus 10 to 15 percent clause in their contracts. You want to make sure to have accurate research for your important decisions.

Timing

- What is the anticipated completion schedule?
- What are the "what if" contingencies? Do they have back-up plans?

Trust

- Remember—quality research firms prosper only if the information they provide helps you to make decisions that improve your company's profitability.
- Once you have selected a professional research group, consider this a partnership; discuss your questions and needs thoroughly with them.

The Marketing Research Process

The basic steps outlined in the following list may be helpful in assigning responsibilities.

Problem Definition

1. Define who is responsible for solving the problem and carrying out the study and recommendations.
2. Set specific objectives for the research project.
3. What is the scope of this study? What is included and excluded from consideration?

Situation Analysis

1. Review the background of the problem as defined in company records and available secondary literature. What is already known about this issue?
2. What are the uncontrollable factors, if any, that affect this problem?
3. What markets are involved?
4. Which of your 4 Ps are affected?

Formal Investigation Steps

1. What information is needed?
2. What sources have that information? What group(s) need to be sampled?
3. What research methods are to be used to gather the information?
4. Design forms and methods for gathering and recording information.
5. Pretest forms for clarity with sample sources.
6. Conduct source sampling.
7. Collect and tabulate data.

Analyze and Interpret Data

1. Summarize data in tables and outlines.
2. Write report(s) of findings.

Problem Solution

1. Present findings with recommendations for action to those responsible for approving and carrying out actions.
2. Follow up to support recommendations.

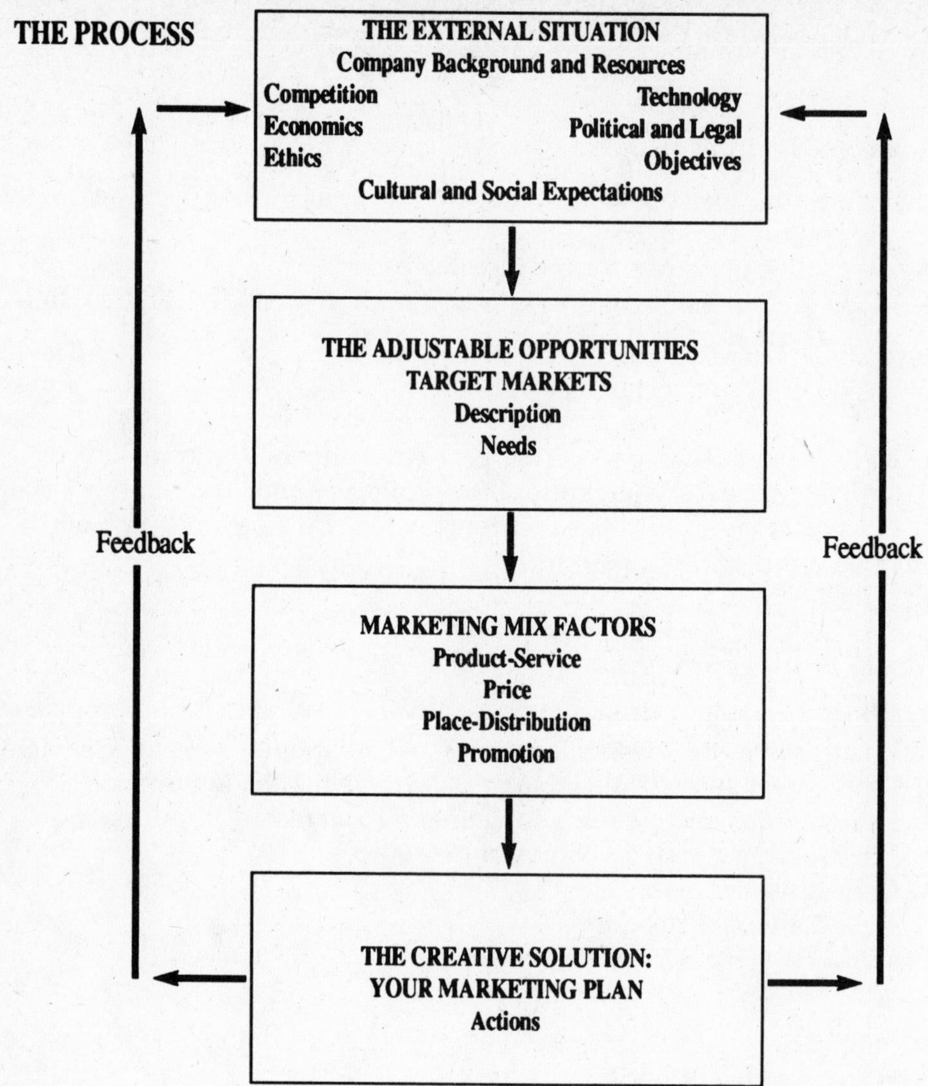

Summary

Marketing research information is particularly important to the marketing planning process because it helps you to identify opportunities, planning directions, and measure the success of your current strategies.

Although marketing research is a tool for decision makers, it cannot make decisions, nor can it substitute for good communication within your company. And remember—useful information is the key word. In this case, more is not necessarily better.

Sources of Information

In this section, we list many research sources and how to access them. Addresses and telephone numbers are subject to change.

Business Publications and Statistical Issues

Most industries have trade publications that specialize in writing about issues and trends affecting the industry. Often they publish annual data in special articles, factbooks, or special issues. Some examples are yearly studies on developments in advertising, appliances, broadcasting, cable television, liquor and cigarette sales, computers, merchandising, drug sales, lumber, farm and industrial equipment, and petroleum. The publishers usually can provide copies of these issues, or copies may be available at the public library. The following directories will help you locate this kind of data:

Business Periodicals Index
H. W. Wilson Co.
950 University Ave.
Bronx, N.Y. 10452
(212) 588-8400

Business Publications Rates and Data
Standard Rate & Data Services, Inc.
3004 Glenview Road
Wilmette, Ill. 60091
(708) 256-6067
Rates and data are also available for community publications, consumer magazines, agri-media, direct mail lists, Hispanic media and markets, newspapers, and spot radio and television.

F & S Index
Predicasts, Inc.
200 University Circle Research Center
1101 Cedar Ave.
Cleveland, Ohio 44106
(216) 795-3000

Ulrich's International Periodicals Directory
R. R. Bowker
Division of Reed Publishing (USA), Inc.
245 W. 17th St.
New York, N.Y. 10011
(800) 346-6049

Commercial Banks and Other Financial Institutions

Large financial institutions need to keep abreast of the economic factors that influence their communities. Your banker or broker can help you tap into this information source. You may want to contact the economic development or public relations officer of the leading bank or financial institution in the city or state you are researching. Other national sources of bank marketing information include:

American Bankers Association
1120 Connecticut Avenue, N.W.
Washington, D.C. 20036
(202) 663-5000

Bank Marketing Association
309 West Washington
Chicago, Ill. 60606
(312) 782-1442

Community Nonprofit Organizations

Organizations such as the United Way, the Red Cross, hospital auxiliaries, community resource centers, museum and zoo groups, drug programs, and major foundations all need factual information about the nation, your region, and your community. In addition, a cross-section of business and volunteer leaders usually sits on their boards of directors; these business leaders believe that their work for such organizations gives them a broader picture of the business environment.

The annual reports, newsletters, funding proposals, and other publications produced by leading nonprofit organizations are good sources for information on trends that affect the external environment of your business. For example, United Way of America has an Environmental Scan Committee, comprised of business, government, and nonprofit managers, that studies a wide range of issues and merges national facts and trends in easy-to-understand publications, videos, slide shows, and graphics. The following publication covers most of the external environment factors that can affect your business.

What Lies Ahead: Countdown to the 21st Century
United Way of America
United Way Strategic Institute
701 Fairfax St.
Alexandria, Va. 22314-2045
(703) 836-7100

Database Publishers

Databases are organized collections of information that are publicly available for lease, license, sale, or search. Some publishers offer data information in both hard copy and electronic format, and some established vendors offer on-line information services for PCs. The early leaders and producers in this twenty-year-old industry were the U.S. National Aeronautics and Space Administration (NASA) and the U.S. Atomic Energy Commission (AEC). Later, academic institutions and other not-for-profit organizations began developing databases for research. In recent years, the for-profit business sector has increased both the number of available databases and the uses for them. Gale Research Inc. estimates that there are now over 5 billion records available for public research purposes!

Consumer database marketing is also known as relationship marketing, one-on-one marketing, relevance marketing, and transactional marketing. As consumer markets have become more specialized and more difficult to reach through the mass media, sophisticated consumer databases have been developed from credit card purchases, warranty card information, questionnaires, preferred customer clubs, and bar-coded coupons. These databases allow your company to pinpoint the preferences and purchase behavior of individual consumers and to track the results of your marketing plans. The databases are expensive to develop and to maintain in-house; however, many companies now provide this service for a fee.

The best place to look for computer databases is in the Computer-Readable Databases, A Directory and Data Sourcebook, published annually by Gale Research Inc. and available in your library or from:

Computer-Readable Databases: A Directory and Data Sourcebook
Gale Research Inc.
835 Penobscot Building
Detroit, Mich. 48226
(800) 877-4253

Government Publications

No one collects more information for and about businesses than the United States government. Two key data terms developed by the government appear in most of the information you will come across: the Metropolitan Statistical Area (MSA) and the Standard Industrial Classification (SIC) codes. The Office of Management and Budget defines a *Metropolitan Statistical Area* as a geographic area with a large population nucleus of at least 50,000 persons, together with adjacent communities that have a high degree of economic and social integration with that nucleus, usually through employment and commuting patterns. A *Standard Industrial Classification* is a system of industrial classification used to categorize businesses by type of economic activity. The codes are published in the Standard Industrial Classification Manual, published by the Executive Office of the President, Office of Management and Budget.

The following are representative of the types of information available through the U.S. Government Printing Office and its bookstores.

- Government Periodicals and Subscription Services, issued quarterly, lists current periodicals and subscriptions alphabetically by title and subject.
- Monthly Catalog of United States Government Publications provides a comprehensive list of federal publications issued each month.
- Monthly Checklist of State Publications records state documents and publications received by the Library of Congress.
- Economic Indicators, issued monthly, is a digest of current information on economic conditions, prices, wages, production, business activity, purchasing power, credit, money, and federal finance, presented in charts and tables.
- Survey of Current Business, also issued monthly, gives information on trends in industry, the business situation, outlook, and other information pertinent to the business world.

The U.S. Government Printing Office operates twenty-four U.S. Government Bookstores that sell more than 21,000 titles directly or through special order. They also stock many free publications. Don't be overwhelmed by the magnitude of "government data"; we have found that the staff members in these offices are very helpful in directing you to the appropriate publications or agencies. The following list may help you find the bookstore nearest you.

Alabama
O'Neill Building
2021 Third Ave., North
Birmingham, AL 35203
(205) 731-1056

California
ARCO Plaza, C-Level
505 South Flower Street
Los Angeles, CA 90071
(213) 894-5841

California
Room 1023, Federal Building
450 Golden Gate Avenue
San Francisco, CA 94102
(415) 556-0643

Colorado
Room 117, Federal Building
1961 Stout Street
Denver, CO 80294
(303) 844-3964

Colorado
World Savings Building
720 North Main Street
Pueblo, CO 81003
(719) 544-3142

District of Columbia
U.S. Government Printing Office
710 North Capitol Street NW
Washington, DC 20401
(202) 275-2091

District of Columbia
1510 H Street NW
Washington, DC 20005
(202) 653-5075

Florida
Room 158, Federal Building
400 W. Bay Street
Jacksonville, FL 32202
(904) 791-3801

Georgia
Room 100, Federal Building
275 Peachtree Street NE
P.O. Box 56445
Atlanta, GA 30343
(404) 331-6947

Illinois
Room 1365, Federal Building
219 S. Dearborn Street
Chicago, IL 60604
(312) 353-5133

Maryland
Warehouse Sales Outlet
8660 Cherry Lane
Laurel, MD 20707
(301) 953-7974
(301) 792-0262

Massachusetts
Thomas P. O'Neill Building
10 Causeway Street, Room 179
Boston, MA 02222
(617) 565-6680

Michigan
Suite 160, Federal Building
477 Michigan Avenue
Detroit, MI 48226
(313) 226-7816

Missouri
120 Bannister Mall
5600 E. Bannister Road
Kansas City, MO 64137
(816) 765-2256

New York
26 Federal Plaza, Room 110
New York, NY 10278
(212) 264-3825

Ohio
Room 1653, Federal Building
1240 E. 9th Street
Cleveland, OH 44199
(216) 522-4922

Ohio
Room 207, Federal Building
200 N. High Street
Columbus, OH 42315
(614) 469-6956

Oregon
1305 S.W. First Avenue
Portland, OR 97201-5801
(503) 221-6217

Texas
Room 1C46, Federal Building
1100 Commerce Street
Dallas, TX 75242
(214) 767-0076

Texas
Texas Crude Building
801 Travis Street, Suite 120
Houston, TX 77002
(713) 653-3100

Washington
Room 194, Federal Building
915 Second Avenue
Seattle, WA 98174
(206) 442-4270

Wisconsin
Room 190, Federal Building
517 E. Wisconsin Avenue
Milwaukee, WI 53202
(414) 297-1304

The Department of Commerce, Bureau of the Census compiles census data, the most extensive statistical data source for information on the United States, its people, and its businesses. The principal functions of this bureau are to collect, tabulate, and publish statistical data, including the following:

- Censuses of Population and Housing (taken every ten years). Proposed subject reports from the 1990 census, which will be available in 1993, include:

Characteristics of Rural and Farm Population
Geographic Mobility for States and the Nation
Geographic Mobility for Metropolitan Areas
Recent and Lifetime Migration
Journey to Work: Metropolitan Commuting Flows
Journey to Work: Characteristics of the Workers in Metropolitan Areas
Place of Work
Detailed Social and Economic Characteristics of the Population
Current Language of the American People
Education
The Older Population of the United States
Persons in Institutions and Other Group Quarters
Households, Families, Marital Status, and Living Arrangements
Fertility
American Indians, Eskimos, and Aleuts in the United States
Characteristics of American Indians by Tribe and Language for Selected Areas
Characteristics of the Asian and Pacific Islander Population in the United States
Characteristics of the Black Population in the United States
Persons of Hispanic Origin in the United States
Ancestry of the Population in the United States
The Foreign-Born Population in the United States
Employment Status, Work Experience, and Veteran Status
Occupational Characteristics
Industrial Characteristics
Occupation by Industry
Earnings by Occupation and Education
Sources and Structure of Household and Family Income
Characteristics of Persons in Poverty
Poverty Areas in the United States

Characteristics of Adults with Work Disabilities, Mobility Limitations, or Self-Care Limitations
Metropolitan Housing Characteristics
Mobile Homes
Recent Mover Households
Housing of the Elderly
Condominium Housing
Structural Characteristics
Utilization of the Housing Stock
Housing Quality Indicators
Second Mortgage Households
Characteristics of New Housing Units

- Censuses of Agriculture, State and Local Governments, Manufacturers, Mineral Industries, Distributive Trades, Construction Industries, and Transportation (taken every five years)

- Monthly, quarterly, and annual surveys that provide current information on many subjects covered in the censuses
- Statistics on U.S. foreign trade (imports, exports, and shipping)
- Estimates and projections of the population
- Current reports on manufacturing, retail and wholesale trade, services, construction, imports and exports, state and local government finances, and employment

The census reference materials as well as sources of assistance, are described in the bureau's catalog/guide, which is available at government bookstores or from:

Census Catalog & Guide
Superintendent of Documents
Government Printing Office
Washington, DC 20402-9325
(202) 783-3238

The Bureau of the Census has excellent reference libraries (and real people to help you) in its twelve regional field offices. You may also contact the Data User Services Division, Bureau of the Census, Department of Commerce, Washington, DC 20233, telephone (301) 763-4100.

The regional offices are located at the following addresses:

California
11777 San Vicente Blvd.
Los Angeles, CA 90049
(213) 575-6612

Colorado
7655 W. Mississippi Ave.
Denver, CO 80226
(303) 969-7750

Georgia
1365 Peachtree St. NE
Atlanta, GA 30309
(404) 347-2274

Illinois
175 W. Jackson Blvd.
Chicago, IL 60604
(312) 353-0980

Kansas
4th and State Sts.
Kansas City, KS
(816) 891-7470

Massachusetts
10 Causeway St.
Boston, MA 02222
(617) 565-7078

Michigan
231 W. Lafayette
Detroit, MI 48226
(313) 226-7742

New York
26 Federal Plaza
New York, NY 10278
(212) 264-3860

North Carolina
222 S. Church St.
Charlotte, NC 28202
(704) 357-8325

Pennsylvania
105 S. 7th St.
Philadelphia, PA 19106
(215) 597-8313

Texas
1100 Commerce St.
Dallas, TX 75242
(214) 767-7105

Washington
Suite 500, 101 Stewart St.
Seattle, WA 98101-7800
(206) 728-5300

The Small Business Administration assists businesses with management issues and provides free information at more than one hundred field offices in cities across the United States. The national office and the ten regional offices are listed below.

Small Business Administration
Imperial Building
1441 L Street NW
Washington, DC 20416
(800) 368-5855

California
450 Golden Gate Ave.
San Francisco, CA 94102
(415) 556-7487

Colorado
Suite 701
999 18th St.
Denver, CO 80202
(303) 294-7001

Georgia
5th Floor
1375 Peachtree St. NE
Atlanta, GA 30367
(404) 347-2797

Illinois
Room 510
230 S. Dearborn St.
Chicago, IL 60604
(312) 353-0359

Massachusetts
10th Floor
60 Batterymarch
Boston, MA 02110
(617) 451-2030

Missouri
13th Floor
911 Walnut St.
Kansas City, MO 64106
(816) 374-5288

New York
Room 31-08
26 Federal Plaza
New York, NY 10278
(212) 264-7772

Pennsylvania
Suite 201
475 Allendale Rd.
King of Prussia, PA 19406
(215) 962-3750

Texas
Building C
8625 King George Dr.
Dallas, TX 75235
(214) 767-7643

Washington
Room 440
2615 4th Ave.
Seattle, WA 98121
(206) 442-5676

Public Library

Some business and product managers tend to discount the business value of the public library. That can be unfortunate, because your local public library, in addition to having important regional and national information, may be your most important source for local and state information. In any town, the public library holds a wealth of information. Talk with the librarian about your questions. Some libraries will fax information to your office for a small fee; others maintain and sell mailing lists of organizations in their service area. Check with your library to learn what services it offers.

Most libraries offer the following basic sources for finding marketing information.

Annual Reports
Complete annual reports, tax reports, and other information supplied to the Securities and Exchange Commission each year by companies listed on the New York and American stock exchanges and traded over the counter. Much of this information is available in library business reference sections.

Commercial Atlas & Marketing Guide
Rand McNally & Company
Skokie, IL 60076-9809
(800) 284-6565
This guide contains maps, tables, and charts providing economic and geographic information and data on the United States population and other statistical business data.

Directory of Corporate Affiliations
International Directory of Corporate Affiliations
National Register Publishing Company
Macmillan Directory Division
3004 Glenview Rd.
Wilmette, IL 60091
(708) 441-2210
These directories list parent companies, their divisions and subsidiaries. They are both indexes of "who owns whom."

Dun's Directories
Dun's Marketing Services
Three Sylvan Way
Parsippany, NJ 07054
(800) 526-0651
The *Million Dollar Directory* series provides facts about decision makers, company size, and lines of business for America's largest companies. The *Regional Business Directories* identify the top firms in retail, wholesale, service, and manufacturing markets for each major metropolitan area. The *Market Profile Analysis* furnishes consumer and business demographics for every metropolitan area and/or county in the United States.

Gale Directory of Publications and Broadcast Media
(formerly *Ayer Directory of Publications*)
Gale Research, Inc.
835 Penobscot Building
Detroit, MI 48226
(800) 877-4253
This publication contains basic information about newspapers, magazines, journals, radio stations, television stations, and cable systems in United States and Canada.

Moody's Industrial Manuals
Moody's Investors Service
The Dun & Bradstreet Corporation
99 Church St.
New York, NY 10007
(800) 342-5647
Moody's various manuals provide detailed directories of industrial, banking and finance, OTC industrial, public utility, transportation, and other corporations. The information includes company history, operations, income statements, and balance sheets, as well as other financial information. Almost all are updated twice a week in specific industry reports.

Standard Directory of Advertisers
Standard Directory of Advertising Agencies
Standard Directory of Worldwide Marketing
National Register Publishing Company
Macmillan Directory Division
3004 Glenview Rd.
Wilmette, IL 60091
(708) 441-2210
These directories, also called the Red Books, list information about companies with annual advertising budgets for national and regional campaigns of over $75,000; information about advertising agencies, their specialties, and personnel; and alphabetic, geographic, and S.I.C. data on international advertisers and agencies, respectively.

Thomas Register of American Manufacturers
Thomas Publishing Company
One Penn Plaza
New York, NY 10001
(212) 695-0500
The Products & Services volumes list all known manufacturers or sources of products or services alphabetically by state and, within each state, by city. The Company Profiles volumes detail capabilities and contact information on U.S. companies. The Catalog File volumes organize detailed product information, including specifications, drawings, photos, availability, and performance data.

Schools

Metro-area School Systems, Trade Schools, Colleges and Universities: All are sources of information about your community and the businesses that serve it. Use their published data (including their course catalogs) as well as their people for resources to help with your marketing needs.

A sophisticated, yet relatively inexpensive university resource example is the BRAIN (Business Research and Information Network) at the University of Colorado. It is a direct link to the NASA Industrial Application Center. Research specialists help access national and international databases, technical files, and expert contacts with federal labs, industry, universities, and private consulting firms.

Business Advancement Centers
University of Colorado
Business Research and Information Network
A NASA Industrial Applications Center Affiliate
1690 38th Street, Suite 101
Boulder, CO 80301
(303) 444-5723
(800) 369-1243

To locate similar services in your area, a guide to university-based and other non-government research organizations in the United States with continuing research programs is available in your library or through the publisher.

Research Centers Directory
Gale Research Inc.
835 Penobscot Building
Detroit, MI 48226
(800) 877-4253

State and Local Chambers of Commerce

Many chambers of commerce offer a variety of services to assist the economic development of their members and their communities. Some of their services include: providing opportunities for networking with other business managers and sponsoring seminars, speakers, trade fairs, booklets, business libraries, and other resource information. Your state and local chambers of commerce or similar organizations are good sources of regional economic, demographic, and statistical data. The U.S. Chamber of Commerce publishes a membership directory, as well as research reports for business use.

U.S. Chamber of Commerce
1615 H Street N.W.
Washington, DC 20062
(202) 659-6000

Some chambers access special markets such as women, minorities, and small businesses. The information they amass can be useful to business managers within those markets, as well as to managers who want to serve or to form coalitions with those markets. The two national umbrella organizations for contacting these special market organizations in local, state, or regional areas are:

National Federation of Independent Business, Inc.
Capitol Gallery East, Suite 700
600 Maryland Avenue S.W.
Washington, DC 20024
(202) 554-9000

National Small Business United
1155 15th Street, N.W., Suite 710
Washington, DC 20005
(202) 293-8830

Telephone Books

Believe it or not, your community telephone book can be your best source of information about your competition and your community. The yellow pages listings and advertisements of your competitors can give you some useful information about their range of services. In addition, the community information pages provide information about the city and areas in which you offer your products and services. Among the other telephone book information that may be valuable if you are unfamiliar with a new location or beginning market development is the following:

- Area codes
- Area history
- Community services directory
- Emergency preparedness procedures
- Entertainment sources
- Government listings
- Higher education resources
- National parks and recreation areas
- Newcomer information
- 900 telephone numbers for business and financial reports
- Sports facilities
- Street guides and maps
- Theater, arena, and stadium seating charts
- Time zone maps
- Transit options
- Voter information
- Zip codes

Trade Associations

Many trade associations maintain research departments and collect basic data on sales, expenses, shipments, stock turnover rates, bad debt losses, collection ratios, returns and allowances, and net operating profits. A modest investment in a membership in your industry's trade association and in the broader associations for marketing and management can provide excellent secondary research sources.

American Management Association
135 West 50th Street
New York, NY 10020
(212) 586-8100

American Marketing Association
250 S. Wacker Drive, Suite 200
Chicago, IL 60606
(312) 648-0536

There are several directories available in the public library that can help you locate specific trade associations. One major source is the Gale Encyclopedia of Associations, available in most libraries or from:

Encyclopedia of Associations
Gale Research Inc.
835 Penobscot Building
Detroit, MI 48226
(800) 877-4253
This directory presents data by categories, as follows:

- *National Organizations of the U.S.*—more than 22,000 national organizations, organized by broad fields such as law, science, business and commerce, medicine, education, sports, hobbies, labor, culture, religion, agriculture, and public affairs.
- *International Organizations*—more than 9,700 nonprofit organizations that are international in scope, membership, or interest.
- *Regional, State, and Local Organizations*—five volumes listing more than 47,000 regional, state, and local organizations such as the Detroit Auto Dealers Association and the California Christmas Tree Growers, as well as regional, state, and local chapters of national groups by regions.
- *CD-ROM Global Access: Associations* (available for electronic use)—more than 78,000 entries for national organizations in the United States; regional, state, and local United States associations; international associations (including multinational and binational groups and national organizations based outside the United States).

Index

[Italic page references refer to figures and tables.]